LITTLE OFFICE
OF THE
BLESSED VIRGIN MARY

LITTLE OFFICE of the BLESSED VIRGIN MARY

Compiled and Edited by

JOHN E. ROTELLE, O.S.A.

Illustrated

CATHOLIC BOOK PUBLISHING CORP.

New Jersey

Nihil Obstat: Daniel V. Flynn, J.C.D.
Censor Librorum

Imprimatur: Patrick J. Sheridan
Vicar General, Archdiocese of New York

This *Little Office of the Blessed Virgin Mary* is excerpted and adapted from the *Liturgy of the Hours*.

(T-450)

ISBN 978-1-947070-37-0
ISBN 978-0-89942-450-7

Printed in Korea 25 WO 1
catholicbookpublishing.com

CONTENTS

FOREWORD

IT is appropriate that this book, *The Little Office of the Blessed Virgin Mary*, appear during the Marian Year of 1987-1988 proclaimed by Pope John Paul II, for such a publication emphasizes the important role of Mary in the life of the Church. From the crucifixion scene to our day devotion to Mary has always been present in the Church one way or another.

The Little Office of Mary began as an abridged office of the Common of the Blessed Virgin Mary, which is found in the *Roman Breviary* and was used on the feasts of Mary. In the early Middle Ages the Little Office was considered a votive office. Just as there was a votive Mass for Our Lady on Saturday so too was there a votive office for her.

In the tenth century there was widespread use of the daily recitation of the Little Office. In the next century Saint Peter Damian reorganized the Little Office and recommended it for daily recitation. By the twelfth century it was used throughout Europe and in some places was obligatory for diocesan and religious clergy with the exception of feast days.

With the reform of the Council of Trent the Little Office was curtailed, and emphasis was placed on the Divine Office, the prayer of the Church. Only certain monastic groups were obliged to recite it daily or otherwise. From the sixteenth century onward, when new congregations of sisters took shape, their common or private prayer was centered on the Little Office. It was during this time that the office became very popular among religious and also began to spread to the laity.

With the liturgical reform of Saint Pius X, once again the Divine Office was emphasized; the Little Office, however, was still added to the Divine Office by many religious orders and congregations. Thus since the Council of Trent this Little Office was primarily a devotional office prayed by congregations of nonclerical religious.

In 1952 the Little Office underwent another revision. This time many new texts had been added: readings, long and short; responsories; antiphons, and prayers. It retained the psalms, canticles, and hymns of the original Little Office.

With the reform of the Divine Office or *Liturgy of the Hours* by the Second Vatican Council the guidelines emphasized that this Little Office had to conform to the general thrust of the Liturgy of the Hours so that it would be a prayer of the Church. Taking this into consideration the revision of the Little Office contained in this book follows the liturgical reform of the Divine Office. The texts for each day of the week are derived from the feasts of Mary as they appear in the *Liturgy of the Hours*. The themes for each day of morning and evening prayer are:

Sunday — Mother of the Church
Monday — Immaculate Conception
Tuesday — Annunciation
Wednesday — Visitation
Thursday — Birth of Jesus
Friday — Sorrowful Mother
Saturday — Assumption

To Morning and Evening Prayer selections from the other liturgical hours have been added: Office of Readings, Daytime Prayer, and Night Prayer. In the appendix are additional prayers.

Those who pray this Little Office join themselves to the prayer of the Church and through Mary unite themselves with that hymn of praise sung throughout all ages in the halls of heaven; they also receive a foretaste of the song of praise in heaven, described by John in the Book of Revelation, the song sung continually before the throne of God and of the Lamb (see General Instruction of the Liturgy of the Hours, 16).

INTRODUCTION

The Little Office has the following hours:

Office of Readings (Matins)
Morning Prayer (Lauds)
Daytime Prayer (Terce, Sext, None)
Evening Prayer (Vespers)
Night Prayer (Compline)

Office of Readings

The Office of Readings provides a richer meditation on sacred scripture and on the outstanding writings of spiritual authors. The office opens with a hymn.

The office has three psalms. A biblical reading follows and then a non-biblical reading usually taken from one of the Fathers or other writers of the Church. The office closes with a prayer or the Song of Praise *(Te Deum)* and a prayer. On Sundays outside of Lent, on the days within the octave of Easter and Christmas, on solemnities and feasts, after the second reading, the *Te Deum* is said; it is omitted at other times.

The Office of Readings may be celebrated at any time during the day or night.

Morning Prayer

Morning Prayer and Evening Prayer are considered the two hinges on which the daily Office turns.

Morning Prayer is arranged as the sanctification of morning. Since this Hour is performed at the break of each new day, it calls to mind the resurrection of the Lord Jesus, the true light who enlightens all people.

This office begins with the introductory verse "God, come to my assistance. Lord, make haste to help me," which is followed by the doxology. Next an appropriate hymn is said.

After the hymn occurs the psalmody, a suitable psalm for morning, then a canticle from the Old Testament, and another psalm of praise.

After the psalmody there is a reading from Scripture. A reading from one of the Fathers or other writers of the Church may be added.

In order to respond to God's word, there is a responsorial verse which can be omitted if need be or replaced by another type of response.

After the gospel canticle (the canticle of Zechariah), which expresses praise and thanksgiving for the redemption, there are prayers to consecrate the day and its work to the Lord. These prayers could be read by one person while the community responds with a refrain, or one person could say the first part, and the community respond with the second part which is indicated by a dash (—). An optional response is also provided. At the end of the petitions there should be time given for personal petitions and silence. Then the *Our Father* is recited by all. The prayer of the day immediately follows.

The celebration concludes with the "May the Lord bless us, etc."

Daytime Prayer

Daytime Prayer is introduced by the verse "God, come to my assistance," with the doxology. Afterward there is psalmody, then a biblical reading and a reading from the Fathers or other writers of the Church, followed by a verse. The Hour is concluded by the prayer and by the acclamation of praise.

Evening Prayer

Evening Prayer is celebrated in the evening so that "we might return thanks for all that was given us, or rightly done by us that day" (St. Basil the Great).

Evening Prayer begins with the introductory verse "God, come to my assistance. Lord, make haste to help me," which is followed by the doxology. Next an appropriate hymn is said.

After the hymn occurs the psalmody, two suitable psalms for evening prayer and a canticle from the New Testament.

After the psalmody there is a reading from Scripture. A reading from one of the Fathers or other writers of the Church may be added.

In order to respond to God's word, there is a responsorial verse which can be omitted if need be or replaced by another type of response.

After the gospel canticle (the canticle of Mary), which expresses praise and thanksgiving for the redemption, there are intercessory prayers. These prayers could be read by one person while the community responds with a refrain, or one person could say the first part, and the community respond with the second part which is indicated by a dash (—). At the end of the petitions there should be time given for personal petitions and silence. Then the *Our Father* is recited by all. The prayer of the day follows.

The celebration concludes with "May the Lord bless and keep us . . . " which is the priestly blessing of Aaron in the Book of Numbers (6:24-26)—a fitting invocation for the close of day.

Night Prayer

Night Prayer is the last prayer of the day said before retiring.

Night Prayer begins with the verse "God, come to my assistance," with the doxology. This is followed by an examination of conscience. A prayer of repentance may be said.

A hymn follows. The psalm used conveys the notion of trust in God.

After the psalmody there is a reading from Scripture. A reading from one of the Fathers or other writers of the Church may be added.

In order to respond to God's word, there is a responsorial verse which can be omitted if need be or replaced by another type of response.

Then comes the gospel canticle (the canticle of Simeon) which is the focal point of the entire Hour.

The concluding prayer follows and then the blessing "May the all-powerful Lord grant us a restful night and a peaceful death. Amen."

Lastly, there is one of the antiphons of the Blessed Virgin Mary.

NOTE

All psalmody is concluded as follows:

Glory to the Father, and to the Son, and to the Holy Spirit:
as it was in the beginning, is now, and will be forever. Amen.

The red dash (—) indicates that the strophe continues on the next page.

SUNDAY

Morning Prayer

God, come to my assistance.
— Lord, make haste to help me.

Glory to the Father, and to the Son, and to the Holy Spirit:
as it was in the beginning, is now, and will be for ever. Amen.

HYMN

O Mary, of all women,
You are the chosen one,
Who, ancient prophets promised,
Would bear God's only Son;
All Hebrew generations
Prepared the way to thee,
That in your womb the God-man
Might come to set man free.

O Mary, you embody
All God taught to our race,
For you are first and foremost
In fullness of his grace;
We praise this wondrous honor
That you gave birth to him
Who from you took his manhood
And saved us from our sin.

Melody: Au fort de ma detresse 76.76D

Music: 17th century
Flemish Melody
Text: Michael Gannon

Or:

Truly, *you are blessed among women.*
For you have changed Eve's curse into a blessing;
and Adam, who hitherto lay under a curse,
has been blessed because of you.

Truly, you are blessed among women.
Through you the Father's blessing has shone forth on mankind,
setting them free of their ancient curse.

Truly, you are blessed among women,
because through you
your forebears have found salvation.
For you were to give birth to the Savior
who was to win them salvation.

Truly, you are blessed among women,
for without seed you have borne, as your fruit,
him who bestows blessings on the whole world
and redeems it from that curse
that made it sprout thorns.

Truly, you are blessed among women,
because, though a woman by nature,
you will become, in reality, God's mother.
If he whom you are to bear is truly God made flesh,
then rightly do we call you God's mother.
For you have truly given birth to God.

Saint Sophronius of Jerusalem (c. 560-638)

Psalmody

Ant. 1 The Virgin has given birth to the Savior; a flower has sprung from Jesse's stock and a star has risen from Jacob. O God, we praise you.

Or: You are all beautiful, O Mary; in you there is no trace of original sin.

Psalm 118

Song of joy for salvation

This Jesus is the stone which, rejected by you builders, has become the chief stone supporting all the rest (Acts 4:11).

Give thanks to the Lord for he is good,
for his love endures for ever.

Let the sons of Israel say:
"His love endures for ever."
Let the sons of Aaron say:
"His love endures for ever."
Let those who fear the Lord say:
"His love endures for ever."

I called to the Lord in my distress;
he answered and freed me.
The Lord is at my side; I do not fear.
What can man do against me?
The Lord is at my side as my helper:
I shall look down on my foes.

It is better to take refuge in the Lord
than to trust in men:
it is better to take refuge in the Lord
than to trust in princes.

The nations all encompassed me;
in the Lord's name I crushed them.
They compassed me, compassed me about;
in the Lord's name I crushed them.
They compassed me about like bees;
they blazed like a fire among thorns.
In the Lord's name I crushed them.

I was hard-pressed and was falling
but the Lord came to help me.
The Lord is my strength and my song;
he is my savior.
There are shouts of joy and victory
in the tents of the just.

The Lord's right hand has triumphed;
his right hand raised me.
The Lord's right hand has triumphed;
I shall not die, I shall live
and recount his deeds.—

I was punished, I was punished by the Lord,
but not doomed to die.

Open to me the gates of holiness:
I will enter and give thanks.
This is the Lord's own gate
where the just may enter.
I will thank you for you have answered
and you are my savior.

The stone which the builders rejected
has become the corner stone.
This is the work of the Lord,
a marvel in our eyes.
This day was made by the Lord;
we rejoice and are glad.

O Lord, grant us salvation;
O Lord, grant success.
Blessed in the name of the Lord
is he who comes.
We bless you from the house of the Lord;
the Lord God is our light.

Go forward in procession with branches
even to the altar.
You are my God, I thank you.
My God, I praise you.
Give thanks to the Lord for he is good;
for his love endures for ever.

Ant. 2 Mary has given birth to our Savior. John the Baptist saw him and cried out: This is the Lamb of God, who takes away the sins of the world.

Or: You are the glory of Jerusalem, the joy of Israel; you are the fairest honor of our race.

Canticle Daniel 3:52-57

Let all creatures praise the Lord

The Creator . . . is blessed for ever (Romans 1:25).

Blessed are you, O Lord, the God of our fathers,
praiseworthy and exalted above all forever.

And blessed is your holy and glorious name,
praiseworthy and exalted above all for all ages.

Blessed are you in the temple of your holy glory,
praiseworthy and glorious above all forever.

Blessed are you on the throne of your kingdom,
praiseworthy and exalted above all forever.

Blessed are you who look into the depths
from your throne upon the cherubim,
praiseworthy and exalted above all forever.

Blessed are you in the firmament of heaven,
praiseworthy and glorious forever.

Bless the Lord, all you works of the Lord,
praise and exalt him above all forever.

Ant. 3 Mary has given birth to a King whose name is everlasting; hers the joy of motherhood, hers the virgin's glory. Never was the like seen before, never shall it be seen again.

Or: The robe you wear is white as spotless snow; your face is radiant like the sun.

Psalm 150

Praise the Lord

Let mind and heart be in your song: this is to glorify God with your whole self (Hesychius).

Praise God in his holy place,
praise him in his mighty heavens.
Praise him for his powerful deeds,
praise his surpassing greatness.

O praise him with sound of trumpet,
praise him with lute and harp.
Praise him with timbrel and dance,
praise him with strings and pipes.

O praise him with resounding cymbals,
praise him with clashing of cymbals.
Let everything that lives and that breathes
give praise to the Lord.

FIRST READING Micah 5:3, 4, 5a

The ruler in Israel will give them up, until the time
when she who is to give birth has borne,
And the rest of his brethren shall return
to the children of Israel.
He shall stand firm and shepherd his flock
by the strength of the Lord,
in the majestic name of the Lord, his God.
He shall be peace.

Or Zephaniah 3:14, 15b

Shout for joy, O daughter Zion!
sing joyfully, O Israel!
Be glad and exult with all your heart,
O daughter Jerusalem!
The King of Israel, the Lord,
is in your midst.

Or Sirach 24:17-21

I bud forth delights like the vine,
my blossoms become fruit fair and rich.
Come to me, all you that yearn for me,
and be filled with my fruits;
You will remember me as sweeter than honey,
better to have than the honeycomb.
He who eats of me will hunger still,
he who drinks of me will thirst for more;
He who obeys me will not be put to shame,
he who serves me will never fail.

Second Reading

From a letter by Saint Athanasius, bishop

(Epist. Ad Epictetum, 5-9; PG 26, 1058, 1062-1066)

The Word took our nature from Mary

What was born of Mary was therefore human by nature, in accordance with the inspired Scriptures, and the body of the Lord was a true body: It was a true body because it was the same as ours. Mary, you see, is our sister, for we are all born from Adam.

The words of Saint John: *The Word was made flesh,* bear the same meaning, as we may see from a similar turn of phrase in Saint Paul: *Christ was made a curse for our sake.* Man's body has acquired something great through its communion and union with the Word. From being mortal it has been made immortal; though it was a living body it has become a spiritual one; though it was made from the earth it has passed through the gates of heaven.

Even when the Word takes a body from Mary, the Trinity remains a Trinity, with neither increase nor decrease. It is for ever perfect. In the Trinity we acknowledge one Godhead, and thus one God, the Father of the Word, is proclaimed in the Church.

Or:

From a sermon by Saint Aelred, abbot

(Sermo 20, in Nativitate beatae Mariae: PL 195, 322-324)

Mary our mother

She is our mother—the mother of our life, the mother of our incarnation, the mother of our light. As the Apostle says of our Lord, *he became for us by God's power our wisdom and justice, and holiness and redemption.*

She then, as mother of Christ, is the mother of our wisdom and justice, of our holiness and redemption.

She is more our mother than the mother of our flesh. Our birth from her is better, for from her is born our holiness, our wisdom, our justice, our sanctification, our redemption.

Praise the Lord in his holy ones, say the Scriptures. If our Lord is to be praised in those holy ones through whom he brings to being deeds of power and miracles, how much more is he to be praised in her in whom he fashioned himself, who is wonderful beyond all wonders.

Or:

From the dogmatic constitution on the Church of the Second Vatican Council

(Lumen gentium, nn. 63-65)

Mary as type of the Church

Mary, because she has entered intimately into the history of salvation, in a certain sense gathers up in her own person the great truths of the faith and awakens their resonance when she is the object of preaching and veneration; she summons the faithful to her Son, to his sacrifice and to the Father's love. In seeking to further the glory of Christ, the Church becomes more and more like Mary, its exalted type, as it continues its progress in faith, hope and charity, seeking and fulfilling the divine will in all things.

So also in its apostolic task the Church rightly looks to the one who bore Christ, Christ who was conceived by the Holy Spirit and born of the Virgin in order that he might also be born and grow in the hearts of the faithful. In her whole life this virgin mother showed herself as an example of that motherly love that must animate all who share in the apostolic mission of the Church for the regeneration of mankind.

RESPONSORY

O Virgin Mary, no other daughter of Jerusalem is your equal,
for you are the mother of the King of kings,
you are the Queen of heaven and of angels.
— Blessed are you among women,
and blessed is the fruit of your womb.

Hail, full of grace; the Lord is with you.
— Blessed are you . . .

Or:

The Word was made man and he lived among us.
— The Word was made man and he lived among us.

He was in the beginning with God,
— and he lived among us.

Glory to the Father . . .
— The Word was . . .

CANTICLE OF ZECHARIAH Luke 1:68-79

Ant. Marvelous is the mystery proclaimed today: man's nature is made new as God becomes man; he remains what he was and becomes what he was not. Yet each nature stays distinct and for ever undivided.

The Messiah and his forerunner

Blessed be the Lord, the God of Israel;
he has come to his people and set them free.

He has raised up for us a mighty savior,
born of the house of his servant David.

Through his holy prophets he promised of old
that he would save us from our enemies,
from the hands of all who hate us.

He promised to show mercy to our fathers
and to remember his holy covenant.

This was the oath he swore to our father Abraham:
to set us free from the hands of our enemies,
free to worship him without fear,
holy and righteous in his sight
all the days of our life.

You, my child, shall be called the prophet of the Most High;
for you will go before the Lord to prepare his way,

to give his people knowledge of salvation
by the forgiveness of their sins.

In the tender compassion of our God
the dawn from on high shall break upon us,
to shine on those who dwell in darkness and the shadow of death,
and to guide our feet into the way of peace.

Glory to the Father, and to the Son, and to the Holy Spirit:
as it was in the beginning, is now, and will be for ever. Amen.

INTERCESSIONS

Let us give glory to Christ who was born of the Virgin Mary by the power of the Holy Spirit, and let us pray to him in these words:
Son of the Virgin Mary, have mercy on us.

Christ, born of the Virgin Mary, you are Wonder-Counselor and Prince of Peace,
— give your peace to the world.

Our King and our God, you have raised us up by your coming,
— help us to honor you all the days of our lives by our faith and our deeds.

You made yourself like us,
— in your mercy grant that we may become more like you.

You made yourself a citizen of our earthly city,
— grant that we may become citizens of our true homeland, your kingdom in heaven.

Our Father . . .

Concluding Prayer

God our Father,
may we always profit by the prayers
of the Virgin Mother Mary,
for you bring us life and salvation
through Jesus Christ her Son
who lives and reigns with you and the Holy Spirit,
one God, for ever and ever.

Alternative Prayer

Father,
source of light in every age,
the virgin conceived and bore your Son
who is called Wonderful God, Prince of Peace.
May her prayer, the gift of a mother's love,
be your people's joy through all ages.
May her response, born of a humble heart,
draw your Spirit to rest on your people.

Grant this through Christ our Lord.

May the Lord bless us,
protect us from all evil
and bring us to everlasting life.
—Amen.

Evening Prayer

God, come to my assistance.
— Lord, make haste to help me.
Glory to the Father, and to the Son, and to the Holy Spirit:
as it was in the beginning, is now, and will be for ever. Amen.

Hymn

Mary the Dawn, Christ the Perfect Day;
Mary the Gate, Christ the Heavenly Way!

Mary the Root, Christ the Mystic Vine;
Mary the Grape, Christ the Sacred Wine!

Mary the Wheat, Christ the Living-Bread;
Mary the Stem, Christ the Rose blood-red!

Mary the Font, Christ the Cleansing Flood;
Mary the Cup, Christ the Saving Blood!

Mary the Temple, Christ the temple's Lord;
Mary the Shrine, Christ the God adored!

Mary the Beacon, Christ the Haven's Rest;
Mary the Mirror, Christ the Vision Blest!

Mary the Mother, Christ the mother's Son
By all things blest while endless ages run. Amen.

Melody: Mary the Dawn Music: Anon.
Irregular

Or:

Your name is Our Lady.
You alone are Mother of God
and raised high over all the earth.
O Spouse of God, we celebrate you with faith,
we honor you with longing,
we venerate you with awe;
at every moment we exalt you
and reverently proclaim you blessed.

Saint Germanus of Constantinople (c. 638-730)

Psalmody

Ant. 1 O marvelous exchange! Man's Creator has become man, born of a virgin. We have been made sharers in the divinity of Christ who humbled himself to share in our humanity.

Or: Mary gave birth to Jesus, who is called the Christ.

Psalm 110:1-5, 7

The Messiah, king and priest

Christ's reign will last until all his enemies are made subject to him (1 Corinthians 15:25).

The Lord's revelation to my Master:
"Sit on my right:
your foes I will put beneath your feet."

The Lord will wield from Zion
your scepter of power:
rule in the midst of all your foes.

A prince from the day of your birth
on the holy mountains;
from the womb before the dawn I begot you.

The Lord has sworn an oath he will not change.
"You are a priest for ever,
a priest like Melchizedek of old."

The Master standing at your right hand
will shatter kings in the day of his great wrath.

He shall drink from the stream by the wayside
and therefore he shall lift up his head.

Ant. 2 By your miraculous birth from the virgin you have fulfilled the Scriptures: like a gentle rain falling upon the earth you have come down to save your people. O God, we praise you.

Or: With the Lord is unfailing love; great is his power to save.

Psalm 112

The happiness of the just man

Live as children born of the light. Light produces every kind of goodness and justice and truth (Ephesians 5:8-9).

Happy the man who fears the Lord,
who takes delight in all his commands.
His sons will be powerful on earth;
the children of the upright are blessed.

Riches and wealth are in his house;
his justice stands firm for ever.
He is a light in the darkness for the upright:
he is generous, merciful and just.

The good man takes pity and lends,
he conducts his affairs with honor.
The just man will never waver:
he will be remembered for ever.

He has no fear of evil news;
with a firm heart he trusts in the Lord.
With a steadfast heart he will not fear;
he will see the downfall of his foes.

Open-handed, he gives to the poor;
his justice stands firm for ever.
His head will be raised in glory.

The wicked man sees and is angry,
grinds his teeth and fades away;
the desire of the wicked leads to doom.

Ant. 3 Your blessed and fruitful virginity is like the bush, flaming yet unburned, which Moses saw on Sinai. Pray for us, Mother of God.

Or: In the beginning, before time began, the Word was God; today he is born, the Savior of the world.

OUTSIDE LENT

Canticle See Revelation 19:1-7

The wedding of the Lamb

Alleluia.
Salvation, glory, and power to our God:
(℟. Alleluia.)—

his judgments are honest and true.
℟. Alleluia (alleluia).

Alleluia.
Sing praise to our God, all you his servants,
(℟. Alleluia.)
all who worship him reverently, great and small.
℟. Alleluia (alleluia).

Alleluia.
The Lord our all-powerful God is King;
(℟. Alleluia.)
let us rejoice, sing praise, and give him glory.
℟. Alleluia (alleluia).

Alleluia.
The wedding feast of the Lamb has begun,
(℟. Alleluia.)
and his bride is prepared to welcome him.
℟. Alleluia (alleluia).

LENT

Canticle 1 Peter 2:21-24

The willing acceptance of his passion by Christ, the servant of God

Ant. For our sakes God made him who did not know sin to be sin, so that in him we might become the very holiness of God.

Christ suffered for you,
and left you an example
to have you follow in his footsteps.

He did no wrong;
no deceit was found in his mouth.
When he was insulted,
he returned no insult.

When he was made to suffer,
he did not counter with threats.
Instead he delivered himself up
to the One who judges justly.

In his own body
he brought your sins to the cross,
so that all of us, dead to sin,
could live in accord with God's will.

By his wounds you were healed.

FIRST READING Galatians 4:4-5

When the fullness of time had come, God sent his Son, born of a woman, born under the law, to ransom those under the law, so that we might receive adoption.

Or Zechariah 9:9a

Rejoice heartily, O daughter Zion,
shout for joy, O daughter Jerusalem.
See, your king shall come to you;
a just savior is he.

Or Revelation 12:1-6

A great sign appeared in the sky, a woman clothed with the sun, with the moon under her feet, and on her head a crown of twelve stars. She was with child and wailed aloud in pain as she labored to give birth. Then another sign appeared in the sky; it was a huge red dragon, with seven heads and ten horns, and on its heads were seven diadems. Its tail swept away a third of the stars in the sky and hurled them down to the earth. Then the dragon stood before the woman about to give birth, to devour her child when she gave birth. She gave birth to a son, a male child, destined to rule all the nations with an iron rod. Her child was caught up to God and his throne. The woman herself fled into the desert where she had a place prepared by God, that there she might be taken care of for twelve hundred and sixty days.

Second Reading

From a sermon by Saint Sophronius, bishop

(Oratio 2, in sanctissimae Deiparae Annuntiatione, 21-22. 26: PG 87, 3, 3242. 3250)

Through Mary the Father's blessing has shone forth on humankind

Hail, full of grace, the Lord is with you. What joy could surpass this, O Virgin Mother? What grace can excel that which God has granted to you alone? What could be imagined more dazzling or more delightful? Before the miracle we witness in you, all else pales; all else is inferior when compared with the grace you have been given. All else, even what is most desirable, must take second place and enjoy a lesser importance.

The Lord is with you. Who would dare challenge you? You are God's mother; who would not immediately defer to you and be glad to accord you a greater primacy and honor? For this reason, when I look upon the privilege you have above all creatures, I extol you with the highest praise: *Hail, full of grace, the Lord is with you.* On your account joy has not only graced men, but is also granted to the powers of heaven.

Responsory

The God of power has given me his strength.
— The God of power has given me his strength.

He has kept me in the way of holiness.
— And has given me his strength.

Glory to the Father . . .
— The God of . . .

Or:

Through you we drink from the wellsprings of salvation, O Blessed Virgin Mary.
—Through you we drink from the wellsprings of salvation, O Blessed Virgin Mary.

From the sacred wounds of Christ,
—O Blessed Virgin Mary.

Glory to the Father . . .
—Through you we . . .

CANTICLE OF MARY Luke 1:46-55

Ant. Blessed is the womb which bore you, O Christ, and the breast that nursed you, Lord and Savior of the world.

My soul rejoices in the Lord

My soul proclaims the greatness of the Lord,
my spirit rejoices in God my Savior
for he has looked with favor on his lowly servant.

From this day all generations will call me blessed:
the Almighty has done great things for me,
and holy is his Name.

He has mercy on those who fear him
in every generation.

He has shown the strength of his arm,
he has scattered the proud in their conceit.

He has cast down the mighty from their thrones,
and has lifted up the lowly.

He has filled the hungry with good things,
and the rich he has sent away empty.

He has come to the help of his servant Israel
for he has remembered his promise of mercy,
the promise he made to our fathers,
to Abraham and his children for ever.

Glory to the Father, and to the Son, and to the Holy Spirit:
as it was in the beginning, is now, and will be for ever. Amen.

Intercessions

To Christ, Emmanuel, whom the Virgin conceived and brought forth, let us give praise and pray to him:
Son of the Virgin Mary, hear us.
You gave Mary the joy of motherhood,
— give all parents true joy in their children.
King of peace, your kingdom is one of justice and peace,
— help us to seek the paths of peace.
You came to make the human race the holy people of God,
— bring all nations to acknowledge the unifying bond of your love.
By your birth you strengthened family ties,
— help families to come to a greater love for one another.
You desired to be born into the days of time,
— grant that our departed brothers and sisters may be born into the day of eternity.

Our Father . . .

Concluding Prayer

God our Father,
may we always profit by the prayers
of the Virgin Mother Mary,
for you bring us life and salvation
through Jesus Christ her Son
who lives and reigns with you and the Holy Spirit,
one God, for ever and ever.

Alternative Prayer

Father,
source of light in every age,
the virgin conceived and bore your Son
who is called Wonderful God, Prince of Peace.
May her prayer, the gift of a mother's love,
be your people's joy through all ages.
May her response, born of a humble heart,
draw your Spirit to rest on your people.

Grant this through Christ our Lord.

May the Lord bless us,
protect us from all evil
and bring us to everlasting life.
 Amen.

MONDAY
Morning Prayer

God, come to my assistance.
— Lord, make haste to help me.
Glory to the Father, and to the Son, and to the Holy Spirit:
as it was in the beginning, is now, and will be for ever. Amen.

HYMN

Mary immaculate, star of the morning,
Chosen before the creation began,
Chosen to bring, for thy bridal adorning,
Woe to the serpent and rescue to man.

Here, in an orbit of shadow and sadness,
Veiling thy splendor, thy course thou hast run;
Now thou art throned in all glory and gladness,
Crowned by the hand of the savior and Son.

Sinners, we worship thy sinless perfection;
Fallen and weak, for thy pity we plead;
Grant us the shield of thy sovereign protection,
Measure thine aid by the depth of our need.

Bend from thy throne at the voice of our crying,
Bend to this earth which thy footsteps have trod;
Stretch out thine arms to us, living and dying,
Mary immaculate, Mother of God.

Melody: Liebster Immanuel 11.10.11.10

Music: Melody from Himmels-Lust, 1679, adapted and harmonized by J. S. Bach
Text: F. W. Weatherell

Or:

Virgin of virgins,
you were untouched by that stain of sin,
that first of all evils,
the sad inheritance of the human race.
From my earliest years
I have placed my hope in you.

Where the power of evil overcomes me
and makes my life too sinful for your gaze,
all the more will your unbounded compassion
show me your generous love,
because my suffering is so deep,
my sinfulness so unworthy of your aid.

Luis de León (1527/1528-1591)

PSALMODY

Ant. 1 O Mother, how pure you are, you are untouched by sin; yours was the privilege to carry God within you.

Or: Blessed are you, O Mary, for the world's salvation came forth from you; now in glory, you rejoice for ever with the Lord. Intercede for us with your Son.

Psalm 90

May we live in the radiance of God

There is no time with God: a thousand years, a single day: it is all one (2 Peter 3:8).

O Lord, you have been our refuge
from one generation to the next.
Before the mountains were born
or the earth or the world brought forth,
you are God, without beginning or end.

You turn men back to dust
and say: "Go back, sons of men."
To your eyes a thousand years
are like yesterday, come and gone,
no more than a watch in the night.

You sweep men away like a dream,
like grass which springs up in the morning.
In the morning it springs up and flowers:
by evening it withers and fades.

So we are destroyed in your anger,
struck with terror in your fury.
Our guilt lies open before you;
our secrets in the light of your face.

All our days pass away in your anger.
Our life is over like a sigh.
Our span is seventy years
or eighty for those who are strong.

And most of these are emptiness and pain.
They pass swiftly and we are gone.
Who understands the power of your anger
and fears the strength of your fury?

Make us know the shortness of our life
that we may gain wisdom of heart.
Lord, relent! Is your anger for ever?
Show pity to your servants.

In the morning, fill us with your love;
we shall exult and rejoice all our days.
Give us joy to balance our affliction
for the years when we knew misfortune.

Show forth your work to your servants;
let your glory shine on their children.
Let the favor of the Lord be upon us:
give success to the work of our hands,
give success to the work of our hands.

Ant. 2 The Lord God Most High has blessed you, Virgin Mary, above all the women of the earth.

Or: You are the glory of Jerusalem, the joy of Israel; you are the fairest honor of our race.

Canticle Isaiah 42:10-16

God victor and savior

They were singing a new hymn before the throne of God (Revelation 14:3).

Sing to the Lord a new song,
his praise from the end of the earth:

Let the sea and what fills it resound,
the coastlands, and those who dwell in them.
Let the steppe and its cities cry out,
the villages where Kedar dwells;

let the inhabitants of Sela exult,
and shout from the top of the mountains.
Let them give glory to the Lord,
and utter his praise in the coastlands.

The Lord goes forth like a hero,
like a warrior he stirs up his ardor;
he shouts out his battle cry,
against his enemies he shows his might:

I have looked away, and kept silence,
I have said nothing, holding myself in;
but now, I cry out as a woman in labor,
gasping and panting.

I will lay waste mountains and hills,
all their herbage I will dry up;
I will turn the rivers into marshes,
and the marshes I will dry up.

I will lead the blind on their journey;
by paths unknown I will guide them.
I will turn darkness into light before them,
and make crooked ways straight.

Ant. 3 Sinless Virgin, let us follow joyfully in your footsteps; draw us after you in the fragrance of your holiness.

Or: O Virgin Mary, how great your cause for joy; God found you worthy to bear Christ our Savior.

Psalm 146

Those who trust in God know what it is to be happy

To praise God in our lives means all we do must be for his glory (Arnobius).

My soul, give praise to the Lord;
I will praise the Lord all my days,
make music to my God while I live.

Put no trust in princes,
in mortal men in whom there is no help.
Take their breath, they return to clay
and their plans that day come to nothing.

He is happy who is helped by Jacob's God,
whose hope is in the Lord his God,
who alone made heaven and earth,
the seas and all they contain.

It is he who keeps faith for ever,
who is just to those who are oppressed.
It is he who gives bread to the hungry,
the Lord, who sets prisoners free,

the Lord who gives sight to the blind,
who raises up those who bowed down,
the Lord, who protects the stranger
and upholds the widow and orphan.

It is the Lord who loves the just
but thwarts the path of the wicked.
The Lord will reign for ever,
Zion's God, from age to age.

FIRST READING — Isaiah 43:1

But now, thus says the Lord,
who created you, O Jacob,
and formed you, O Israel:
Fear not, for I have redeemed you;
I have called you by name: you are mine.

OR — Galatians 4:4-5

When the fullness of time had come, God sent his Son, born of a woman, born under the law, to ransom those under the law, so that we might receive adoption.

Or Proverbs 8:22-31

Mary in the mind of God

The Lord begot me, the firstborn of his ways,
  the forerunner of his prodigies of long ago;
From of old I was poured forth,
  at the first, before the earth.
When there were no depths I was brought forth,
  when there were no foundations or springs of water;
Before the mountains were settled into place,
  before the hills, I was brought forth;
While as yet the earth and the fields were not made,
  nor the first clods of the world.

When he established the heavens I was there,
  when he marked out the vault over the face of the deep;
When he made firm the skies above,
  when he fixed fast the foundations of the earth;
When he set for the sea its limit,
  so that the waters should not transgress his command;
Then was I beside him as his craftsman,
  and I was his delight day by day,
Playing before him all the while,
  playing on the surface of his earth;
  and I found delight in the sons of men.

Second Reading

From a sermon by Saint Anselm, bishop

(Oratio 52: PL 158, 955-956)

Virgin Mary, all nature is blessed in you

Blessed Lady, sky and stars, earth and rivers, day and night—everything that is subject to the power or use of man—rejoice that through you they are in some sense restored to their lost beauty and are endowed with inexpressible new grace. All creatures were dead, as it were, useless for human beings or for the praise of God, who made them. The world, contrary to its true destiny, was corrupted and tainted by the acts of human beings who served idols. Now all creation has been restored to life and rejoices that it is controlled and given splendor by those who believe in God.

The universe rejoices with new and indefinable loveliness. Not only does it feel the unseen presence of God himself, its Creator, it sees him openly, working and making it holy. These great blessings spring from the blessed fruit of Mary's womb.

Through the fullness of the grace that was given you, dead things rejoice in their freedom, and those in heaven are glad to be made new. Through the Son who was the glorious fruit of your virgin womb, just souls who died before his life-giving death rejoice as they are freed from captivity, and the angels are glad at the restoration of their shattered domain.

Lady, full and overflowing with grace, all creation received new life from your abundance. Virgin, blessed above all creatures, through your blessing all creation is blessed, not only creation from its Creator, but the Creator himself has been blessed by creation.

To Mary God gave his only-begotten Son, whom he loved as himself. Through Mary God made himself a Son, not different but the same, by nature Son of God and Son of Mary. The whole universe was created by God, and God was born of Mary. God created all things, and Mary gave birth to God. The God who made all things gave himself form through Mary, and thus he made his own creation. He who could create all things from nothing would not remake his ruined creation without Mary.

God, then, is the Father of the created world and Mary the mother of the re-created world. God is the Father by whom all things were given life, and Mary the mother through whom all things were given new life. For God begot the Son, through whom all things were made, and Mary gave birth to him as the Savior of the world. Without God's Son, nothing could exist; without Mary's Son, nothing could be redeemed.

Truly the Lord is with you, to whom the Lord granted that all nature should owe as much to you as to himself.

RESPONSORY

The God of power has given me his strength.
— The God of power has given me his strength.

He has kept me in the way of holiness.
— And has given me his strength.

Glory to the Father . . .
— The God of . . .

Or:

O Virgin Mary, no other daughter of Jerusalem is your equal,
for you are the mother of the King of kings,
you are the Queen of heaven and of angels.
— Blessed are you among women,
and blessed is the fruit of your womb.

Hail, full of grace; the Lord is with you.
— Blessed are you . . .

CANTICLE OF ZECHARIAH Luke 1:68-79

Ant. The Lord God said to the serpent: I will make you enemies, you and the woman, your offspring and her offspring; she will crush your head, alleluia.

Or: Holy Mary, ever-virgin, Mother of God, blessed are you among women and blessed is the fruit of your womb.

The Messiah and his forerunner

Blessed be the Lord, the God of Israel;
he has come to his people and set them free.

He has raised up for us a mighty savior,
born of the house of his servant David.

Through his holy prophets he promised of old
that he would save us from our enemies,
from the hands of all who hate us.

He promised to show mercy to our fathers
and to remember his holy covenant.

This was the oath he swore to our father Abraham:
to set us free from the hands of our enemies,
free to worship him without fear,
holy and righteous in his sight
all the days of our life.

You, my child, shall be called the prophet of the Most High;
for you will go before the Lord to prepare his way,

to give his people knowledge of salvation
by the forgiveness of their sins.

In the tender compassion of our God
the dawn from on high shall break upon us,
to shine on those who dwell in darkness and the shadow of death,
and to guide our feet into the way of peace.

Glory to the Father, and to the Son, and to the Holy Spirit:
as it was in the beginning, is now, and will be for ever. Amen.

INTERCESSIONS

Let us glorify our Savior, who chose the Virgin Mary for his mother. Let us ask him:
May your mother intercede for us, Lord.

Sun of Justice, the Immaculate Virgin was the white dawn announcing your rising,
— grant that we may always live in the light of your coming.

Savior of the world, by your redeeming might you preserved your mother beforehand from all stain of sin,
— keep watch over us, lest we sin.

You are our redeemer, who made the Immaculate Virgin Mary your purest home and the sanctuary of the Holy Spirit,
— make us temples of your Spirit for ever.
King of kings, you lifted up your mother, body and soul, into heaven;
— help us to fix our thoughts on things above.

Our Father . . .

Concluding Prayer

Father,
you prepared the Virgin Mary
to be the worthy mother of your Son.
You let her share beforehand
in the salvation Christ would bring by his death,
and kept her sinless from the first moment of her conception.
Help us by her prayers
to live in your presence without sin.
We ask this through our Lord Jesus Christ, your Son,
who lives and reigns with you and the Holy Spirit,
one God, for ever and ever.

Alternative Prayer

Father,
the image of the Virgin is found in the Church.
Mary had a faith that your Spirit prepared
and a love that never knew sin,
for you kept her sinless from the first moment of her conception.
Trace in our actions the lines of her love,
in our hearts her readiness of faith.
Prepare once again a world for your Son
who lives and reigns with you and the Holy Spirit,
one God, for ever and ever.

May the Lord bless us,
protect us from evil

and bring us to everlasting life.
— Amen.

Evening Prayer

God, come to my assistance.
— Lord make haste to help me.
Glory to the Father, and to the Son, and to the Holy Spirit:
as it was in the beginning, is now, and will be for ever. Amen.

HYMN

Mary, crowned with living light,
Temple of the Lord,
Place of peace and holiness,
Shelter of the Word.

Mystery of sinless life
In our fallen race.
Free from shadow, you reflect
Plenitude of grace.

Virgin-Mother of our God,
Lift us when we fall,
Who were named upon the Cross
Mother of us all.

Father, Son and Holy Ghost,
Heaven sings your praise;
Mary magnifies your name
Through eternal days.

Melody: Glorification 75.75.D — Music: Gossner's *Choralbuch*, Leipzig, 1882
Text: Stanbrook Abbey

Or:

Salve, Regina, mater misericordiae;
vita, dulcedo et spes nostra, salve.
Ad te clamamus, exsules filii Evae,
Ad te suspiramus, gementes et flentes
in hac lacrimarum valle.

Eia ergo, advocata nostra,
illos tuos misericordes oculos
ad nos converte.
Et Iesum, benedictum fructum ventris tui,
nobis post hoc exsilium ostende.
O clemens, o pia, o dulcis Virgo Maria.

Melody: Salve Regina — Music: Paris, 1634
Text: 11th century

Psalmody

Ant. 1 You are all beautiful, O Mary; in you there is no trace of original sin.

Or: Mary received a blessing from the Lord and loving kindness from God her savior.

Psalm 136

Easter hymn

We praise God by recalling his marvelous deeds (Cassiodorus).

I

O give thanks to the Lord for he is good,
for his love endures for ever.
Give thanks to the God of gods,
for his love endures for ever.
Give thanks to the Lord of lords,
for his love endures for ever;

who alone has wrought marvellous works,
for his love endures for ever;
whose wisdom it was made the skies,
for his love endures for ever;
who fixed the earth firmly on the seas,
for his love endures for ever.

It was he who made the great lights,
for his love endures for ever,
the sun to rule in the day,
for his love endures for ever, —

the moon and stars in the night,
for his love endures for ever.

Ant. 2 You are the glory of Jerusalem, the joy of Israel; you are the fairest honor of our race.

Or: The Most High has made his dwelling place a holy temple.

II

The first-born of the Egyptians he smote,
for his love endures for ever.
He brought Israel out from their midst,
for his love endures for ever;
arm outstretched, with power in his hand,
for his love endures for ever.

He divided the Red Sea in two,
for his love endures for ever;
he made Israel pass through the midst,
for his love endures for ever;
he flung Pharaoh and his force in the sea,
for his love endures for ever.

Through the desert his people he led,
for his love endures for ever.
Nations in their greatness he struck,
for his love endures for ever.
Kings in their splendor he slew,
for his love endures for ever.

Sihon, king of the Amorites,
for his love endures for ever;
and Og, the king of Bashan,
for his love endures for ever.

He let Israel inherit their land,
for his love endures for ever.
On his servant their land he bestowed,
for his love endures for ever.
He remembered us in our distress,
for his love endures for ever.

And he snatched us away from our foes,
for his love endures for ever.
He gives food to all living things,
for his love endures for ever.
To the God of heaven give thanks,
for his love endures for ever.

Ant. 3 The robe you wear is white as spotless snow;
your face is radiant like the sun.

Or: Glorious things are said of you, O Virgin Mary.

Canticle Ephesians 1:3-10

God our Savior

Praised be the God and Father
of our Lord Jesus Christ,
who has bestowed on us in Christ
every spiritual blessing in the heavens.

God chose us in him
before the world began
to be holy
and blameless in his sight,
to be full of love.

He predestined us
to be his adopted sons through Jesus Christ,
such was his will and pleasure,
that all might praise the glorious favor
he has bestowed on us in his beloved.

In him and through his blood, we have been redeemed,
and our sins forgiven,
so immeasurably generous
is God's favor to us.

God has given us the wisdom
to understand fully the mystery,
the plan he was pleased
to decree in Christ.

A plan to be carried out
in Christ, in the fullness of time,
to bring all things into one in him,
in the heavens and on earth.

FIRST READING Romans 5:20-21

Where sin increased, grace overflowed all the more, so that, as sin reigned in death, grace also might reign through justification for eternal life through Jesus Christ our Lord.

OR Ephesians 5:25-27

Christ loved the church and handed himself over for her to sanctify her, cleansing her by the bath of water with the word, that he might present to himself the church in splendor, without spot or wrinkle or any such thing, that she might be holy and without blemish.

OR James 3:13-18

Who among you is wise and understanding? Let him show his works by a good life in the humility that comes from wisdom. But if you have bitter jealousy and selfish ambition in your hearts, do not boast and be false to the truth. Wisdom of this kind does not come down from above but is earthly, unspiritual, demonic. For where jealousy and selfish ambition exist, there is disorder and every foul practice. But the wisdom from above is first of all pure, then peaceable, gentle, compliant, full of mercy and good fruits, without inconstancy or insincerity. And the fruit of righteousness is sown in peace for those who cultivate peace.

SECOND READING

From a homily delivered at the Council of Ephesus by Saint Cyril of Alexandria, bishop
(Hom. 4: PG 77, 991.995-996)

In praise of Mary, Mother of God

Mary, Mother of God, we salute you. Precious vessel, worthy of the whole world's reverence, you are an ever-shining light, the crown of virginity, the symbol of orthodoxy, an indestructible temple, the place that held him whom no place can contain, mother and virgin. Because of you the holy gospels could say: *Blessed is he who comes in the name of the Lord.*

We salute you, for in your holy womb he, who is beyond all limitation, was confined. Because of you the holy Trinity is glorified and adored; the cross is called precious and is venerated throughout the world; the heavens exult; the angels and archangels make merry; demons are put to flight; the devil, that tempter, is thrust down from heaven; the fallen race of man is taken up on high; all creatures possessed by the madness of idolatry have attained knowledge of the truth; believers receive holy baptism; the oil of gladness is poured out; the Church is established throughout the world; pagans are brought to repentance.

What more is there to say? Because of you the light of the only-begotten Son of God has shone upon those who sat in darkness and in the shadow of death; prophets pronounced the word of God; the apostles preached salvation to the Gentiles; the dead are raised to life, and kings rule by the power of the holy Trinity.

RESPONSORY

By this I know you have chosen me.
— By this I know you have chosen me.

You have not let my enemy triumph over me.
— You have chosen me.

Glory to the Father . . .
— By this I . . .

Or:

I shall glorify you, Lord, for you have rescued me.
— I shall glorify you, Lord, for you have rescued me.

You have not let my enemies rejoice over me.
— For you have rescued me.

Glory to the Father . . .
— I shall glorify . . .

CANTICLE OF MARY Luke 1:46-55

Ant. Hail Mary, full of grace; the Lord is with you; blessed are you among women, and blessed is the fruit of your womb, alleluia.

Or: All generations will call me blessed: the Almighty has done great things for me.

My soul rejoices in the Lord

My soul proclaims the greatness of the Lord,
my spirit rejoices in God my Savior
for he has looked with favor on his lowly servant.

From this day all generations will call me blessed:
the Almighty has done great things for me,
and holy is his Name.

He has mercy on those who fear him
in every generation.

He has shown the strength of his arm,
he has scattered the proud in their conceit.

He has cast down the mighty from their thrones,
and has lifted up the lowly.

He has filled the hungry with good things,
and the rich he has sent away empty.

He has come to the help of his servant Israel
for he has remembered his promise of mercy,
the promise he made to our fathers,
to Abraham and his children for ever.

Glory to the Father, and to the Son, and to the Holy Spirit:
as it was in the beginning, is now, and will be for ever. Amen.

Intercessions

Let us praise God our almighty Father, who wished that Mary, his Son's mother, be celebrated by each generation. Now in need we ask:
Mary, full of grace, intercede for us.

O God, worker of miracles, you made the immaculate Virgin Mary share, body and soul, in your Son's glory in heaven,
— direct the hearts of your children to that same glory.

You made Mary our mother. Through her intercession grant strength to the weak, comfort to the sorrowing, pardon to sinners,
— salvation and peace to all.

You made Mary the mother of mercy,
— may all who are faced with trials feel her motherly love.

You wished Mary to be the mother of the family in the home of Jesus and Joseph,
— may all mothers of families foster love and holiness through her intercession.

You crowned Mary queen of heaven,
— may all the dead rejoice in your kingdom with the saints for ever.

Our Father . . .

Concluding Prayer

Father,
you prepared the Virgin Mary
to be the worthy mother of your Son.
You let her share beforehand
in the salvation Christ would bring by his death,
and kept her sinless from the first moment of her conception.
Help us by her prayers
to live in your presence without sin.

We ask this through our Lord Jesus Christ, your Son,
who lives and reigns with you and the Holy Spirit,
one God, for ever and ever.

Alternative Prayer

Father,
the image of the Virgin is found in the Church.
Mary had a faith that your Spirit prepared
and a love that never knew sin,
for you kept her sinless from the first moment of her conception.
Trace in our actions the lines of her love,
in our hearts her readiness of faith.
Prepare once again a world for your Son
who lives and reigns with you and the Holy Spirit,
one God, for ever and ever.

May the Lord bless us,
protect us from evil
and bring us to everlasting life.
—Amen.

TUESDAY

Morning Prayer

God, come to my assistance.
— Lord, make haste to help me.
Glory to the Father, and to the Son, and to the Holy Spirit:
as it was in the beginning, is now, and will be for ever. Amen.

HYMN

Mother of Christ, our hope, our Patroness,
Star of the sea, our beacon in distress,
Guide to the shores of everlasting day
God's holy people on their pilgrim way.

Virgin by vow but Mother of all grace,
Chosen by God to be his dwelling-place,
Blessed are you: God's word you did believe,
Your "Yes" undid the "No" of sinful Eve.

Daughter of God, who bore his holy One,
Dearest of all, the Christ, your loving Son,
Show us his face, O Mother, as on earth,
Loving us all, you gave our Savior birth.

Melody: Farley Castle 10.10.10.10
Music: H. Lawes, 1596-1662
Text: *Alma Redemptoris*
Translator: James Quinn, S.J.

Or:

Behold then the joy of the whole universe.
Let the union of God and man in the Son of the Virgin Mary
fill us with awe and adoration.
Let us fear and worship the undivided Trinity
as we sing the praise of the ever-virgin Mary,
the holy temple of God,

and of God himself, her Son and spotless Bridegroom.
To him be glory for ever and ever. Amen.

Saint Cyril of Alexandria (c. 382-444)

PSALMODY

Ant. 1 The angel Gabriel was sent to the Virgin Mary, who was engaged to be married to Joseph.

Or: Blessed are you, O Virgin Mary, for you carried the Creator of the world in your womb.

Psalm 101

Avowal of a good ruler

If you love me, keep my commandments (John 14:15).

My song is of mercy and justice;
I sing to you, O Lord.
I will walk in the way of perfection.
O when, Lord, will you come?

I will walk with blameless heart
within my house;
I will not set before my eyes
whatever is base.

I will hate the ways of the crooked;
they shall not be my friends.
The false-hearted must keep far away;
the wicked I disown.

The man who slanders his neighbor in secret
I will bring to silence.
The man of proud looks and haughty heart
I will never endure.

I look to the faithful in the land
that they may dwell with me.
He who walks in the way of perfection
shall be my friend.

No man, who practices deceit
shall live within my house.—

No man who utters lies shall stand
before my eyes.

Morning by morning I will silence
all the wicked in the land,
uprooting from the city of the Lord
all who do evil.

Ant. 2 Blessed are you among women, and blessed is the fruit of your womb.

Or: You are the mother of your Maker, yet you remain a virgin for ever.

Canticle Daniel 3:26, 27, 29, 34-41

Azariah's prayer in the furnace

With your whole hearts turn to God and he will blot out all your sins (Acts 3:19).

Blessed are you, and praiseworthy,
O Lord, the God of our fathers,
and glorious forever is your name.

For you are just in all you have done;
all your deeds are faultless, all your ways right,
and all your judgments proper.

For we have sinned and transgressed
by departing from you,
and we have done every kind of evil.

For your name's sake, do not deliver us up forever,
or make void your covenant.

Do not take away your mercy from us,
for the sake of Abraham, your beloved,
Isaac your servant, and Israel your holy one,

to whom you promised to multiply their offspring
like the stars of heaven,
or the sand on the shore of the sea.

For we are reduced, O Lord, beyond any other nation,
brought low everywhere in the world this day
because of our sins.

We have in our day no prince, prophet, or leader,
no holocaust, sacrifice, oblation, or incense,
no place to offer first fruits, to find favor with you.

But with contrite heart and humble spirit
let us be received;
as though it were holocausts of rams and bullocks,
or thousands of fat lambs,
so let our sacrifice be in your presence today
as we follow you unreservedly;
for those who trust in you cannot be put to shame.

And now we follow you with our whole heart,
we fear you and we pray to you.

Ant. 3 Trusting in the Lord's promise, the Virgin Mary conceived a child, and remaining a virgin, she gave birth to the Savior.

Or: We share the fruit of life through you, O daughter blessed by the Lord.

Psalm 135:1-12

Praise for the wonderful things God does for us

He has won you for himself . . . and you must proclaim what he has done for you: he has called you out of darkness into his own wonderful light (1 Peter 2:9).

Praise the name of the Lord,
praise him, servants of the Lord,
who stand in the house of the Lord,
in the courts of the house of our God.

Praise the Lord for the Lord is good.
Sing a psalm to his name for he is loving.
For the Lord has chosen Jacob for himself
and Israel for his own possession.

For I know the Lord is great,
that our Lord is high above all gods.
The Lord does whatever he wills,
in heaven, on earth, in the seas.

He summons clouds from the ends of the earth;
makes lightning produce the rain;
from his treasuries he sends forth the wind.

The first-born of the Egyptians he smote,
of man and beast alike.
Signs and wonders he worked
in the midst of your land, O Egypt,
against Pharaoh and all his servants.

Nations in their greatness he struck
and kings in their splendor he slew.
Sihon, king of the Amorites,
Og, the king of Bashan,
and all the kingdoms of Canaan.
He let Israel inherit their land;
on his people their land he bestowed.

First Reading — Philippians 2:6-7

Though he was in the form of God,
Jesus did not regard equality with God something to be grasped.
Rather, he emptied himself,
taking the form of a slave,
coming in human likeness,
and found human in appearance,

Or — Sirach 24:1-16

Wisdom sings her own praises,
before her own people she proclaims her glory;

In the assembly of the Most High she opens her mouth,
in the presence of his hosts she declares her worth!

"From the mouth of the Most High I came forth,
  and mistlike covered the earth.
In the highest heavens did I dwell,
  my throne on a pillar of cloud.
The vault of heaven I compassed alone,
  through the deep abyss I wandered.
Over the waves of the sea, over all the land,
  over every people and nation I held sway.
Among all these I sought a resting place;
  in whose inheritance should I abide?

"Then the Creator of all gave me his command,
  and he who formed me chose the spot for my tent,
Saying, 'In Jacob make your dwelling,
  in Israel your inheritance.'
Before all ages, in the beginning, he created me,
  and through all ages I shall not cease to be.
In the holy tent I ministered before him,
  and in Zion I fixed my abode.
Thus in the chosen city he has given me rest,
  in Jerusalem is my domain.
I have struck root among the glorious people,
  in the portion of the Lord, his heritage.

"Like a cedar on Lebanon I am raised aloft,
  like a cypress on Mount Hermon,
Like a palm tree in Engedi,
  like a rosebush in Jericho,
Like a fair olive tree in the field,
  like a plane tree growing beside the water.
Like cinnamon, or fragrant balm, or precious myrrh,
  I give forth perfume;
Like galbanum and onycha and sweet spices,
  like the odor of incense in the holy place.
I spread out my branches like a terebinth,
  my branches so bright and so graceful."

Second Reading

From a sermon by Saint Leo the Great, pope

(Sermo 1 in Nativitate Domini, 2. 3: PL 54, 191-192)

Mary conceived in her soul before she conceived in her body

A royal virgin of the house of David is chosen. She is to bear a holy child, one who is both God and man. She is to conceive him in her soul before she conceives him in her body. In the face of so unheard of an event she is to know no fear through ignorance of the divine plan; the angel tells her what is to be accomplished in her by the Holy Spirit. She believes that there will be no loss of virginity, she who is soon to be the mother of God.

Why should she lose heart at this new form of conceiving when she has been promised that it will be effected through the power of the Most High? She believes, and her faith is confirmed by the witness of a previous wonder: against all expectation Elizabeth is made fruitful. God has enabled a barren woman to be with child; he must be believed when he makes the same promise to a virgin.

Responsory

Hail Mary, full of grace, the Lord is with you.
— Hail Mary, full of grace, the Lord is with you.

Blessed are you among women, and blessed is the fruit of your womb.
— The Lord is with you.

Glory to the Father . . .
— Hail Mary, full . . .

Or:

After the birth of your son, you remained a virgin.
— After the birth of your son, you remained a virgin.

Mother of God, intercede for us;
— you remained a virgin.

Glory to the Father . . .
— After the birth . . .

CANTICLE OF ZECHARIAH Luke 1:68-79

Ant. In his great love for us, God sent his Son in the likeness of our sinful nature.

The Messiah and his forerunner

Blessed be the Lord, the God of Israel;
he has come to his people and set them free.

He has raised up for us a mighty savior,
born of the house of his servant David.

Through his holy prophets he promised of old
that he would save us from our enemies,
from the hands of all who hate us.

He promised to show mercy to our fathers
and to remember his holy covenant.

This was the oath he swore to our father Abraham:
to set us free from the hands of our enemies,
free to worship him without fear,
holy and righteous in his sight
all the days of our life.

You, my child, shall be called the prophet of the Most High;
for you will go before the Lord to prepare his way,

to give his people knowledge of salvation
by the forgiveness of their sins.

In the tender compassion of our God
the dawn from on high shall break upon us,
to shine on those who dwell in darkness and the shadow of death,
and to guide our feet into the way of peace.

Glory to the Father, and to the Son, and to the Holy Spirit:
as it was in the beginning, is now, and will be for ever. Amen.

Intercessions

We celebrate the beginning of our salvation when the coming of the Lord was announced by the angel. Let us pray with joy in our hearts, saying:
May God's holy Mother intercede for us.

Mary received God's word with joy,
— may joy fill our hearts as we welcome our Savior.

You looked with love on your lowly servant,
— in your mercy, Father, remember us and all your children.

Mary, the new Eve, was obedient to your word,
— may we echo her loving obedience.

May God's holy Mother help all in distress, encourage the fainthearted, console the sorrowful,
— may she pray for your holy people, for the clergy, and for all women dedicated to your service.

Our Father . . .

Concluding Prayer

God our Father,
your Word became man and was born of the Virgin Mary.
May we become more like Jesus Christ,
whom we acknowledge as our redeemer, God and man.

We ask this through our Lord Jesus Christ, your Son,
who lives and reigns with you and the Holy Spirit,
one God, for ever and ever.

May the Lord bless us,
protect us from evil
and bring us to everlasting life.
— Amen.

Evening Prayer

God, come to my assistance.
— Lord, make haste to help me.

Glory to the Father, and to the Son, and to the Holy Spirit:
as it was in the beginning, is now, and will be for ever. Amen.

HYMN

Mary occupies a place in the Church which is highest after Christ
and yet very close to us
for you chose her to give the world
that very Life which renews all things,
Jesus Christ, your Son and our Lord.

And so we praise you, Mary, virgin and mother.
After the Savior himself, you alone are all holy,
free from the stain of sin,
gifted by God from the first instant of your conception
with a unique holiness.

Mary, free from all sin and led by the Holy Spirit,
you embraced God's saving will with a full heart,
and devoted yourself totally as a handmaid of the Lord
to the fulfillment of his will in your life,
and to the mystery of our redemption.

Mary, your privileged and grace-filled origin
is the Father's final step in preparing humanity
to receive its Redeemer in human form.

Your fullness of grace is the Father's sign of his favor to the Church
and also his promise to the Church
of its perfection as the Bride of Christ,
radiant in beauty.
Your holiness in the beginning of your life
is the foreshadowing of that all-embracing holiness
with which the Father will surround his people
when his Son comes at the end of time to greet us.

Book of Mary, NCCB

Or:

Mary, we turn with confidence to you,
who are always ready to listen with a mother's affection
and powerful assistance.

Consoler of the afflicted,
Health of the sick,
Refuge of sinners,
grant us comfort in tribulation,
relief in sickness,
and liberating strength in our weakness.

You who are free from sin, lead us to combat sin.
Obtain for us the victory of hope over anguish,
of joy and beauty over boredom and disgust,
of eternal visions over temporal ones,
of life over death.
Mary, conceived without sin,
pray for us who have recourse to you.

Book of Mary, NCCB

PSALMODY

Ant. 1 The angel of the Lord brought God's message to Mary. And she conceived by the power of the Holy Spirit.

Or: Blessed are you, O Mary, for the world's salvation came forth through you; now in glory, you rejoice for ever with the Lord.

Psalm 137:1-6

By the rivers of Babylon

The Babylonian captivity is a type of our spiritual captivity (Saint Hilary).

By the rivers of Babylon
there we sat and wept,
remembering Zion;
on the poplars that grew there
we hung up our harps.

For it was there that they asked us,
our captors, for songs,
our oppressors, for joy.
"Sing to us," they said,
"one of Zion's songs."

O how could we sing
the song of the Lord
on alien soil?
If I forget you, Jerusalem,
let my right hand wither!

O let my tongue
cleave to my mouth
if I remember you not,
if I prize not Jerusalem
above all my joys!

Ant. 2 Do not be afraid, Mary; you have found favor with God. Behold you shall conceive and bear a son, and he will be called the Son of the Most High.

Or: The Lord has chosen her, his loved one from the beginning. He has taken her to live with him.

Psalm 138
Thanksgiving

The kings of the earth will bring his glory and honor into the holy city (see Revelation 21:24).

I thank you, Lord, with all my heart,
you have heard the words of my mouth.
In the presence of the angels I will bless you.
I will adore before your holy temple.

I thank you for your faithfulness and love
which excel all we ever knew of you.
On the day I called, you answered;
you increased the strength of my soul.

All earth's kings shall thank you
when they hear the words of your mouth.
They shall sing of the Lord's ways:
"How great is the glory of the Lord!"

The Lord is high yet he looks on the lowly
and the haughty he knows from afar.
Though I walk in the midst of affliction
you give me life and frustrate my foes.

You stretch out your hand and save me,
your hand will do all things for me.
Your love, O Lord, is eternal.
discard not the work of your hands.

Ant. 3 I am the handmaid of the Lord. Let it be done to me as you have said.

Or: The Lord made you so glorious that your praise will never cease to resound among men.

Canticle Revelation 4:11; 5:9, 10, 12

Redemption hymn

O Lord our God, you are worthy
to receive glory and honor and power.

For you have created all things;
by your will they came to be and were made.

Worthy are you, O Lord,
to receive the scroll and break open its seals.

For you were slain;
with your blood you purchased for God
men of every race and tongue,
of every people and nation.

You made of them a kingdom,
and priests to serve our God,
and they shall reign on the earth.

Worthy is the Lamb that was slain
to receive power and riches,
wisdom and strength,
honor and glory and praise.

FIRST READING 1 John 1:1-2

What was from the beginning,
what we have heard,
what we have seen with our eyes,
what we looked upon
and touched with our hands
concerns the Word of life—
for the life was made visible;
we have seen it and testify to it
and proclaim to you the eternal life
that was with the Father and was made visible to us.

Or Ephesians 2:12-22

You were strangers to the covenants of promise, without hope and without God in the world. But now in Christ Jesus you who once were far off have become near by the blood of Christ.

For he is our peace, he who made both one and broke down the dividing wall of enmity, through his flesh, abolishing the law with its commandments and legal claims, that he might create in himself one new person in place of the two, thus establishing peace, and might reconcile both with God, in one body, through the cross, putting that enmity to death by it. He came and preached peace to you who were far off and peace to those who were near, for through him we both have access in one Spirit to the Father.

So then you are no longer strangers and sojourners, but you are fellow citizens with the holy ones and members of the household of God, built upon the foundation of the apostles and prophets, with Christ Jesus himself as the capstone. Through him the whole structure is held together and grows into a temple sacred in the Lord; in him you also are being built together into a dwelling place of God in the Spirit.

Second Reading

From a sermon by Saint Augustine, bishop
(Sermo 25, 7-8: PL 46, 937-938)

She who believed by faith, conceived by faith

Stretching out his hand over his disciples, the Lord Christ declared: *Here are my mother and my brothers, anyone who does the will of my Father who sent me is my brother and my sister and my mother.* I would urge you to ponder these words. Did the Virgin Mary, who believed by faith and conceived by faith, who was the chosen one from whom our Savior was born among men, who was created by Christ before Christ was created in her—did she not do the will of the Father?

Indeed the blessed Mary certainly did the Father's will, and so it was for her a greater thing to have been Christ's disciple than to have been his mother, and she was more blessed in her discipleship than in her motherhood. Hers was the happiness of first bearing in her womb him whom she would obey as her master.

RESPONSORY

The Word was made man and he lived among us.
— The Word was made man and he lived among us.

He was in the beginning with God,
— and he lived among us.

Glory to the Father . . .
— The Word was . . .

Or:

The Lord has chosen her,
his loved one from the beginning.
— The Lord has chosen her,
his loved one from the beginning.

He has taken her to live with him,
— his loved one from the beginning.

Glory to the Father . . .
— The Lord has . . .

CANTICLE OF MARY Luke 1:46-55

Ant. The angel Gabriel said to Mary in greeting: Hail, full of grace, the Lord is with you; blessed are you among women.

My soul rejoices in the Lord

My soul proclaims the greatness of the Lord,
my spirit rejoices in God my Savior
for he has looked with favor on his lowly servant.

From this day all generations will call me blessed:
the Almighty has done great things for me,
and holy is his Name.

He has mercy on those who fear him
in every generation.

He has shown the strength of his arm,
he has scattered the proud in their conceit.

He has cast down the mighty from their thrones,
and has lifted up the lowly.

He has filled the hungry with good things,
and the rich he has sent away empty.

He has come to the help of his servant Israel
for he has remembered his promise of mercy,
the promise he made to our fathers,
to Abraham and his children for ever.

Glory to the Father, and to the Son, and to the Holy Spirit:
as it was in the beginning, is now, and will be for ever. Amen.

Intercessions

On this day the eternal Father sent his angel to bring to Mary the good news of our salvation. Let us turn to God and pray with confidence:
Lord, fill our hearts with your love.

You chose the Virgin Mary as the mother of your Son,
— have mercy on all who look for your gift of salvation.

You sent Gabriel to give Mary your message of peace and joy,
— give to the whole world the joy of salvation and your gift of true peace.

Mary gave her consent, the Holy Spirit overshadowed her, and your Word came to dwell among us,
— touch our hearts, that we may welcome Christ as Mary did.

You look with love on the humble, and fill the hungry with your gifts,
— raise up the downcast, help all in need, comfort and strengthen the dying.

Lord our God, you alone work wonders and with you all things are possible,
— give us the fullness of salvation when you raise up the dead on the last day.

Our Father . . .

CONCLUDING PRAYER

God our Father,
your Word became man and was born of the Virgin Mary.
May we become more like Jesus Christ,
whom we acknowledge as our redeemer, God and man.

We ask this through our Lord Jesus Christ, your Son,
who lives and reigns with you and the Holy Spirit,
one God, for ever and ever.

May the Lord bless us,
protect us from evil
and bring us to everlasting life.
—Amen.

WEDNESDAY

Morning Prayer

God, come to my assistance.
— Lord, make haste to help me.
Glory to the Father, and to the Son, and to the Holy Spirit:
as it was in the beginning, is now, and will be for ever. Amen.

HYMN

O Mary, of all women
Thou art the chosen one,
Who ancient prophets promised
Would bear God's only Son;
All Hebrew generations
Prepared the way to thee,
That in your womb the God-man
Might come to set man free.

O Mary, you embody
All God taught to our race,
For you are first and foremost
In fullness of his grace;
We praise this wondrous honor
That you gave birth to him
Who from you took his manhood
And saved us from our sin.

Melody: Au fort de ma detresse 76.76.D

Music: 17th century Flemish Melody
Text: Michael Gannon

Or:

I bow before you, Virgins of virgins,
resting-place of the divine Bridegroom,
temple of eternal Wisdom,
sanctuary of the Holy Spirit,
palace of the Blessed Trinity,

Mother full of love and tenderness,
fountain of beauty,
wellspring of wonders,
golden key of God's kingdom,
you are the admiration of angels,
the joy of the human family.
Who can ever do justice to your glory,
to your Queenship of grace?

Eugenio Cantera (1880-1955)

Psalmody

Ant. 1 Mary arose and went with haste into the hill country, to a town of Judah.

Or: Blessed are you, O Virgin Mary, for you carried the Creator of the world in your womb.

Psalm 108

Praise of God and a plea for help

Since the Son of God has been exalted above the heavens, his glory is proclaimed through all the earth (Arnobius).

My heart is ready, O God;
I will sing, sing your praise.
Awake, my soul;
awake, lyre and harp.
I will awake the dawn.

I will thank you, Lord, among the peoples,
among the nations I will praise you,
for your love reaches to the heavens
and your truth to the skies.

O God, arise above the heavens;
may your glory shine on earth!

O come and deliver your friends;
help with your right hand and reply.
From his holy place God has made this promise:
"I will triumph and divide the land of Shechem;
I will measure out the valley of Succoth.

Gilead is mine and Manasseh.
Ephraim I take for my helmet,
Judah for my commander's staff.
Moab I will use for my washbowl,
on Edom I will plant my shoe.
Over the Philistines I will shout in triumph."

But who will lead me to conquer the fortress?
Who will bring me face to face with Edom?
Will you utterly reject us, O God,
and no longer march with our armies?

Give us help against the foe:
for the help of man is vain.
With God we shall do bravely
and he will trample down our foes.

Ant. 2 When Elizabeth heard Mary's greeting, the infant in her womb leaped for joy, and she was filled with the Holy Spirit.

Or: Blessed are you among women, and blessed is the fruit of your womb.

Canticle — Isaiah 61:10—62:5

The prophet's joy in the vision of a new Jerusalem

I saw the holy city, new Jerusalem, with the beauty of a bride adorned for her husband (Revelation 21:2).

I rejoice heartily in the Lord,
in my God is the joy of my soul;
for he has clothed me with a robe of salvation,
and wrapped me in a mantle of justice,
like a bridegroom adorned with a diadem,
like a bride bedecked with her jewels.

As the earth brings forth its plants,
and a garden makes its growth spring up,
so will the Lord God make justice and praise
spring up before all the nations.

For Zion's sake I will not be silent,
for Jerusalem's sake I will not be quiet,
until her vindication shines forth like the dawn
and her victory like a burning torch.

Nations shall behold your vindication,
and all kings your glory;
you shall be called by a new name
pronounced by the mouth of the Lord.
You shall be a glorious crown in the hand of the
Lord,
a royal diadem held by your God.

No more shall men call you "Forsaken,"
or your land "Desolate,"
but you shall be called "My delight,"
and your land "Espoused."
For the Lord delights in you,
and makes your land his spouse.

As a young man marries a virgin,
your Builder shall marry you;
and as a bridegroom rejoices in his bride
so shall your God rejoice in you.

Ant. 3 Blessed are you, Mary, because you believed that the Lord's words to you would be fulfilled.

Or: We share the fruit of life through you, O daughter blessed by the Lord.

Psalm 144:1-10

Prayer for victory and peace

I can do all things in him who strengthens me (Philippians 4:13).

Blessed be the Lord, my rock,
who trains my arms for battle,
who prepares my hands for war.

He is my love, my fortress;
he is my stronghold, my savior,
my shield, my place of refuge.
He brings peoples under my rule.

Lord, what is man that you care for him,
mortal man, that you keep him in mind;
man, who is merely a breath,
whose life fades like a passing shadow?

Lower your heavens and come down;
touch the mountains; wreathe them in smoke.
Flash your lightnings; rout the foe,
shoot your arrows and put them to flight.

Reach down from heaven and save me;
draw me out from the mighty waters,
from the hands of alien foes
whose mouths are filled with lies,
whose hands are raised in perjury.

To you, O God, will I sing a new song;
I will play on the ten-stringed harp
to you who give kings their victory,
who set David your servant free.

FIRST READING Joel 2:27—3:1a

You shall know that I am in the midst of Israel;
  I am the Lord, your God, and there is no other;
  my people shall nevermore be put to shame.
Then afterward I will pour out
  my spirit upon all mankind.
Your sons and daughters shall prophesy.

Or Song of Songs 2:8-14

Hark! my lover—here he comes
  springing across the mountains,
  leaping across the hills.

My lover is like a gazelle
  or a young stag.
Here he stands behind our wall,
  gazing through the windows,
  peering through the lattices.
My lover speaks; he says to me,
  "Arise, my beloved, my beautiful one,
  and come!

"For see, the winter is past,
  the rains are over and gone.
The flowers appear on the earth,
  the time of pruning the vines has come,
  and the song of the dove is heard in our land.
The fig tree puts forth its figs,
  and the vines, in bloom, give forth fragrance.
Arise, my beloved, my beautiful one,
  and come!

"O my dove in the clefts of the rock,
  in the secret recesses of the cliff,
Let me see you,
  let me hear your voice,
For your voice is sweet,
  and you are lovely."

Second Reading

From the Encyclical Letter *Redemptoris Mater* of Pope John Paul II

(Number 36, 25 March 1987)

The whole salvific economy is concentrated in the Mother of Christ

When Elizabeth greeted her young kinswoman coming from Nazareth, *Mary replied with the Magnificat*. In her greeting, Elizabeth first called Mary "blessed" because of "the fruit of her womb," and then she called her "blessed" because of her faith. These two blessings referred directly to the Annunciation. Now, at the Visitation, when Elizabeth's greeting bears witness to that culminating moment, Mary's faith acquires a new consciousness and a new expression. That which remained hidden in the depths of the "obedience of faith" at the Annunciation can now be said to spring forth like a clear and life-giving flame of the spirit.

The words used by Mary on the threshold of Elizabeth's house are *an inspired profession of her faith,* in which *her response to the revealed word* is expressed with the religious and poetical exultation of her whole being toward God. In these sublime words, which are simultaneously very simple and wholly inspired by the sacred texts of the people of Israel, Mary's personal experience, the ecstasy of her heart, shines forth. In them shines a ray of the mystery of God, the glory of his ineffable holiness, the eternal *love which, as an irrevocable gift, enters into human history.*

Mary is the first to share in this new revelation of God and, within the same, in this new "self-giving" of God. Therefore she proclaims: "For he who is mighty has done great things for me, and holy is his name." Her words reflect a joy of spirit which is difficult to express: "My spirit rejoices in God my Savior." Indeed, "the deepest truth about God and the salvation of man is made clear to us in Christ, who is at the same time the mediator and the fullness of all revelation."

In her exultation Mary confesses that she finds herself *in the very heart of this fullness* of Christ. She is conscious that the promise made to the fathers, first of all "to Abraham and to his posterity for ever," is being fulfilled in herself. She is thus aware that concentrated within herself as the Mother of Christ is *the whole salvific economy,* in which "from age to age" is manifested he who, as the God of the Covenant, "remembers his mercy."

RESPONSORY

The Lord has chosen her,
his loved one from the beginning.
— The Lord had chosen her,
his loved one from the beginning.

He has taken her to live with him,
— his loved one from the beginning.

Glory to the Father . . .
— The Lord has . . .

Or:

Hail Mary, full of grace, the Lord is with you.
— Hail Mary, full of grace, the Lord is with you.

Blessed are you among women, and blessed is the fruit
of your womb.
— The Lord is with you.

Glory to the Father . . .
— Hail Mary, full . . .

CANTICLE OF ZECHARIAH — Luke 1:68-79

Ant. When Elizabeth heard Mary's greeting, she cried out and said: Who am I that the mother of my Lord should come to me?

The Messiah and his forerunner

Blessed be the Lord, the God of Israel;
he has come to his people and set them free.

He has raised up for us a mighty savior,
born of the house of his servant David.

Through his holy prophets he promised of old
that he would save us from our enemies,
from the hands of all who hate us.

He promised to show mercy to our fathers
and to remember his holy covenant.

This was the oath he swore to our father Abraham:
to set us free from the hands of our enemies,
free to worship him without fear,
holy and righteous in his sight
all the days of our life.

You, my child, shall be called the prophet of the Most High;
for you will go before the Lord to prepare his way,

to give his people knowledge of salvation
by the forgiveness of their sins.

In the tender compassion of our God
the dawn from on high shall break upon us,
to shine on those who dwell in darkness and the shadow of death,
and to guide our feet into the way of peace.

Glory to the Father, and to the Son, and to the Holy Spirit:
as it was in the beginning, is now, and will be for ever. Amen.

INTERCESSIONS

Let us glorify our Savior, who chose the Virgin Mary for his mother. Let us ask him:
May your mother intercede for us, Lord.

Sun of Justice, the immaculate Virgin was the white dawn announcing your rising,
— grant that we may always live in the light of your coming.

Lord, help us imitate Mary, your mother, who chose the best part,
— may we seek the food that will sustain us for ever.

Savior of the world, by your redeeming might you preserved your mother beforehand from all stain of sin,
— keep watch over us, lest we sin.

You are our redeemer, who made the immaculate Virgin Mary your purest home and the sanctuary of the Holy Spirit,
— make us temples of your Spirit for ever.

Our Father . . .

CONCLUDING PRAYER

Eternal Father,
you inspired the Virgin Mary, mother of your Son,
to visit Elizabeth and assist her in her need.
Keep us open to the working of your Spirit,
and with Mary may we praise you for ever.

We ask this through our Lord Jesus Christ, your Son,
who lives and reigns with you and the Holy Spirit,
one God, for ever and ever.

May the Lord bless us,
protect us from evil
and bring us to everlasting life.
— Amen.

Evening Prayer

God, come to my assistance.
— Lord, make haste to help me.
Glory to the Father, and to the Son, and to the Holy Spirit:
as it was in the beginning, is now, and will be for ever. Amen.

HYMN

What joy,
what happiness there is in heaven!

The shoot from the root of Jesse,
sown so long ago
in the time of the patriarchs,
has today sprung up and begun to grow.

It will bear a Flower
which is destined to heal the world,
a Flower whose scent revives the dead,
whose taste heals the sick,
and whose beauty delights the angels—
a white and red Flower
which angels long to see.

Thomas of Villanova (1487-1555)

Or:

Look upon Mary, my beloved,
how, when Gabriel entered in to her
and she spoke with him words of enquiry:
"How shall these things be?"
and the minister of the Spirit gave reply
to Mary and said: "It is easy for God,
all things are simple for him"—
how she held it true when she heard, and said:
"Behold, his handmaid am I."

Therefore he came down, in a manner he knows,
he stirred and came in a way that pleased him,
he entered and dwelt in her without her perceiving,
she received him, suffering nothing.
He was in her womb like a babe,
yet the whole world was full of him.
Of his love he came down to renew
the image of Adam grown old.

Saint Ephrem (c. 306-373)

Or:

Ave Maria, gratia plena, Dominus tecum,
benedicta tu in mulieribus,
et benedictus fructus ventris tui, Jesu.
Sancta Maria, Mater Dei,
ora pro nobis peccatoribus,
nunc et in hora mortis nostrae. Amen.

Melody: Ave Maria, Gregorian Model I

Music: Traditional, Gregorian
Text: Traditional

PSALMODY

Ant. 1 Mary entered the house of Zechariah, and greeted Elizabeth.

Or: Blessed are you, O Mary, for the world's salvation came forth from you; now in glory, you rejoice for ever with the Lord. Intercede for us with your Son.

Psalm 139:1-18, 23-24

God sees all that is

Who has known the mind of God, who has been his counselor? (Romans 11:34).

I

O Lord, you search me and you know me,
you know my resting and my rising,
you discern my purpose from afar.
You mark when I walk or lie down,
all my ways lie open to you.

Before ever a word is on my tongue
you know it, O Lord, through and through.
Behind and before you besiege me,
your hand ever laid upon me.
Too wonderful for me, this knowledge,
too high, beyond my reach.

O where can I go from your spirit,
or where can I flee from your face?
If I climb the heavens, you are there.
If I lie in the grave, you are there.

If I take the wings of the dawn
and dwell at the sea's furthest end,
even there your hand would lead me,
your right hand would hold me fast.

If I say: "Let the darkness hide me
and the light around me be night,"
even darkness is not dark for you
and the night is as clear as the day.

Ant. 2 When your greeting sounded in my ears, the infant in my womb leaped for joy.

Or: The Lord God Most High has blessed you, Virgin Mary, above all the women of the earth.

II

For it was you who created my being,
knit me together in my mother's womb.
I thank you for the wonder of my being,
for the wonders of all your creation.

Already you knew my soul,
my body held no secret from you
when I was being fashioned in secret
and molded in the depths of the earth.

Your eyes saw all my actions,
they were all of them written in your book;
every one of my days was decreed
before one of them came into being.

To me, how mysterious your thoughts,
the sum of them not to be numbered!
If I count them, they are more than the sand;
to finish, I must be eternal, like you.

O search me, God, and know my heart.
O test me and know my thoughts.
See that I follow not the wrong path
and lead me in the path of life eternal.

Ant. 3 Blessed are you among women, and blessed is the fruit of your womb.

Or: Sinless Virgin, let us follow joyfully in your footsteps; draw us after you in the fragrance of your holiness.

Canticle Colossians 1:12-20

Christ the first-born of all creation
and the first-born from the dead

Let us give thanks to the Father
for having made you worthy
to share the lot of the saints
in light.

He rescued us
from the power of darkness
and brought us
into the kingdom of his beloved Son.
Through him we have redemption,
the forgiveness of our sins.

He is the image of the invisible God,
the first-born of all creatures.
In him everything in heaven and on earth was created,
things visible and invisible.

All were created through him;
all were created for him.
He is before all else that is.
In him everything continues in being.

It is he who is head of the body, the church!
he who is the beginning,
the first-born of the dead,
so that primacy may be his in everything.

It pleased God to make absolute fullness reside in him
and, by means of him, to reconcile everything in his person,
both on earth and in the heavens,
making peace through the blood of his cross.

First Reading — 1 Peter 5:5b-7

Clothe yourselves with humility in your dealings with one another, for:

"God opposes the proud
but bestows favor on the humble."

So humble yourselves under the mighty hand of God, that he may exalt you in due time. Cast all your worries upon him because he cares for you.

Or Colossians 3:12-17

Put on then, as God's chosen ones, holy and beloved, heartfelt compassion, kindness, humility, gentleness, and patience, bearing with one another and forgiving one another, if one has a grievance against another; as the Lord has forgiven you, so must you also do. And over all these put on love, that is, the bond of perfection. And let the peace of Christ control your hearts, the peace into which you were also called in one body. And be thankful. Let the word of Christ dwell in you richly, as in all wisdom you teach and admonish one another, singing psalms, hymns, and spiritual songs with gratitude in your hearts to God. And whatever you do, in word or in deed, do everything in the name of the Lord Jesus, giving thanks to God the Father through him.

SECOND READING

From a homily by Saint Bede the Venerable, priest
(Lib 1, 4: CCL 122, 25-26. 30)

Mary proclaims the greatness of the Lord working in her

My soul proclaims the greatness of the Lord, and my spirit rejoices in God my savior. With these words Mary first acknowledges the special gifts she has been given. Then she recalls God's universal favors, bestowed unceasingly on the human race.

When a man devotes all his thoughts to the praise and service of the Lord, he proclaims God's greatness. His observance of God's commands, moreover, shows that he has God's power and greatness always at heart. His spirit rejoices in God his savior and delights in the mere recollection of his creator who gives him hope for eternal salvation.

These words are often for all God's creations, but especially for the Mother of God. She alone was chosen, and she burned with spiritual love for the son she so joyously conceived. Above all other saints, she alone could truly rejoice in Jesus, her savior, for she knew that he who was the source of eternal salvation would be born in time in her body, in one person both her own son and her Lord.

For the Almighty has done great things for me, and holy is his name. Mary attributes nothing to her own merits. She refers all her greatness to the gift of the one whose essence is power and whose nature is greatness, for he fills with greatness and strength the small and the weak who believe in him.

She did well to add: *and holy is his name,* to warn those who heard, and indeed all who would receive his words, that they must believe and call upon his name. For they too could share in everlasting holiness and true salvation according to the words of the prophet: *and it will come to pass, that everyone who calls on the name of the Lord will be saved.* This is the name she spoke of earlier: *and my spirit rejoices in God my savior.*

Therefore it is an excellent and fruitful custom of holy Church that we should sing Mary's hymn at the time of evening prayer. By meditating upon the incarnation, our devotion is kindled, and by remembering the example of God's Mother, we are encouraged to lead a life of virtue. Such virtues are best achieved in the evening. We are weary after the day's work and worn out by our distractions. The time for rest is near, and our minds are ready for contemplation.

Responsory

Hail Mary, full of grace, the Lord is with you.
— Hail Mary, full of grace, the Lord is with you.

Blessed are you among women, and blessed is the fruit of your womb.
— The Lord is with you.

Glory to the Father . . .
— Hail Mary, full of grace, the Lord is with you.

Or — Luke 1:45, 46; Psalm 66:16

Happy are you who have believed,
because the Lord's promises will be accomplished in you.
And Mary said:
— My soul proclaims the greatness of the Lord.

Come, and listen,
and I will tell what great things God has accomplished for me.
— My soul proclaims . . .

CANTICLE OF MARY — Luke 1:46-55

Ant. All generations will call me blessed; the Lord has looked with favor on his lowly servant.

My soul rejoices in the Lord

My soul proclaims the greatness of the Lord,
my spirit rejoices in God my Savior
for he has looked with favor on his lowly servant.

From this day all generations will call me blessed:
the Almighty has done great things for me,
and holy is his Name.

He has mercy on those who fear him
in every generation.

He has shown the strength of his arm,
he has scattered the proud in their conceit.

He has cast down the mighty from their thrones,
and has lifted up the lowly.

He has filled the hungry with good things,
and the rich he has sent away empty.

He has come to the help of his servant Israel
for he has remembered his promise of mercy,
the promise he made to our fathers,
to Abraham and his children for ever.

Glory to the Father, and to the Son, and to the Holy Spirit:
as it was in the beginning, is now, and will be for ever. Amen.

INTERCESSIONS

Let us praise God our almighty Father, who wished that Mary, his Son's mother, be celebrated by each generation. Now in need we ask:
Mary, full of grace, intercede for us.

O God, worker of miracles, you made the Immaculate Virgin Mary share body and soul in your Son's glory in heaven,
— direct the hearts of your children to that same glory.

Lord, make your Church one in mind and heart, united in your love,
— and keep Christians united in prayer with Mary, the mother of Jesus.

You made Mary the mother of mercy,
— may all who are faced with trials feel her motherly love.

You wished Mary to be the mother of the family in the home of Jesus and Joseph,
— may all mothers of families foster love and holiness through her intercession.

You crowned Mary queen of heaven,
— may all the dead rejoice in your kingdom with the saints for ever.

Our Father . . .

Concluding Prayer

Eternal Father,
you inspired the Virgin Mary, mother of your Son,
to visit Elizabeth and assist her in her need.
Keep us open to the working of your Spirit,
and with Mary may we praise you for ever.

We ask this through our Lord Jesus Christ, your Son,
who lives and reigns with you and the Holy Spirit,
one God, for ever and ever.

May the Lord bless us,
protect us from evil
and bring us to everlasting life.
—Amen.

THURSDAY

Morning Prayer

God, come to my assistance.
— Lord, make haste to help me.
Glory to the Father, and to the Son, and to the Holy Spirit:
as it was in the beginning, is now, and will be for ever. Amen.

HYMN

Virgin born, we bow before you;
Blessed was the womb that bore you;
Mary, Mother meek and mild,
Blessed was she in her Child.
Blessed was the maid that fed you;
Blessed was the hand that led you;
Blessed was the parent's eye
That watched your slumbering infancy.

Blessed she by all creation,
Who brought forth the world's salvation;
And blessed they forever blest,
Who love you most and serve you best.
Virgin born, we bow before you:
Blessed was the womb that bore you;
Mary, Mother meek and mild,
Blessed was she in her Child.

Melody: Mon Dieu, Prete Moi L'Oreille 88-77.D (Genevan Psalm 86) — Music: *Genevan Psalter*, 1543; Text: R. Heber, 1783-1826, alt.

Or:

Holy Virgin Mary, Mother of God,
I come before you, unworthy as I am,
to renew our total dedication to you,

Be now and for ever
our Mother, our advocate and our protector;
rule over us as our sovereign Lady,
keep us from falling,
but if we do fall
help us to rise again without delay.
Show yourself as Mother of God,
to whom all sinners have been entrusted:
be our patroness and theirs
with your loving Son.

Jeanne-Joseph du Vieux-Châtel
(1724-1797)

Psalmody

Ant. 1 Tell us, shepherds, what have you seen? Who has appeared on earth? We have seen a newborn infant and a choir of angels praising the Lord.

Or: O Mother, how pure you are, you are untouched by sin; yours was the privilege to carry God within you.

Psalm 143:1-11

Prayer in distress

A man is not justified by observance of the law but only through faith in Jesus Christ (Galatians 2:16).

Lord, listen to my prayer:
turn your ear to my appeal.
You are faithful, you are just; give answer.
Do not call your servant to judgment
for no one is just in your sight.

The enemy pursues my soul;
he has crushed my life to the ground;
he has made me dwell in darkness
like the dead, long forgotten.
Therefore my spirit fails;
my heart is numb within me.

I remember the days that are past:
I ponder all your works.
I muse on what your hand has wrought
and to you I stretch out my hands.
Like a parched land my soul thirsts for you.

Lord, make haste and answer;
for my spirit fails within me.
Do not hide your face
lest I become like those in the grave.

In the morning let me know your love
for I put my trust in you.
Make me know the way I should walk;
to you I lift up my soul.

Rescue me, Lord, from my enemies;
I have fled to you for refuge.
Teach me to do your will
for you, O Lord, are my God.
Let your good spirit guide me
in ways that are level and smooth.

For your name's sake, Lord, save my life;
in your justice save my soul from distress.

Ant. 2 The angel said to the shepherds: I proclaim to you a great joy; today the Savior of the world is born for you.

Or: You are the glory of Jerusalem, the joy of Israel; you are the fairest honor of our race.

Canticle — Isaiah 66:10-14a

Joys of heaven

The heavenly Jerusalem is a free woman and our mother (Galatians 4:26).

Rejoice with Jerusalem and be glad because of her,
all you who love her;

exult, exult with her,
all you who were mourning over her!

Oh, that you may suck fully
of the milk of her comfort,
that you may nurse with delight
at her abundant breasts!

For thus says the Lord:
Lo, I will spread prosperity over her like a river,
and the wealth of the nations like an overflowing
torrent.

As nurslings, you shall be carried in her arms,
and fondled in her lap;
as a mother comforts her son,
so will I comfort you;
in Jerusalem you shall find your comfort.

When you see this, your heart shall rejoice,
and your bodies flourish like the grass.

Ant. 3 A little child is born for us today; little and yet called the mighty God.

Or: O Virgin Mary, how great your cause for joy; God found you worthy to bear Christ our Savior.

Psalm 147:1-11

The loving kindness of God who can do all he wills

You are God: we praise you; you are the Lord: we acclaim you.

Praise the Lord for he is good;
sing to our God for he is loving:
to him our praise is due.

The Lord builds up Jerusalem
and brings back Israel's exiles,
he heals the broken-hearted,
he binds up all their wounds.
He fixes the number of the stars;
he calls each one by its name.

Our Lord is great and almighty;
his wisdom can never be measured.
The Lord raises the lowly;
he humbles the wicked to the dust.
O sing to the Lord, giving thanks;
sing psalms to our God with the harp.

He covers the heavens with clouds;
he prepares the rain for the earth,
making mountains sprout with grass
and with plants to serve man's needs.
He provides the beasts with their food
and young ravens that call upon him.

His delight is not in horses
nor his pleasure in warriors' strength.
The Lord delights in those who revere him,
in those who wait for his love.

First Reading — Hebrews 1:1-2

In times past, God spoke in partial and various ways to our ancestors through the prophets; in these last days, he spoke to us through a son, whom he made heir of all things and through whom he created the universe.

Or — Titus 2:11-12

For the grace of God has appeared, saving all and training us to reject godless ways and worldly desires and to live temperately, justly, and devoutly in this age.

Or — Songs of Songs 6:9-10

One alone is my dove, my perfect one,
her mother's chosen,
the dear one of her parent.
The daughters saw her and declared her fortunate,
the queens and concubines, and they sang her praises;

Who is this that comes forth like the dawn,
as beautiful as the moon, as resplendent as the sun,
as awe-inspiring as bannered troops?

SECOND READING

From a sermon by Saint Thomas of Villanova, bishop
(Sermon on the Birth of Mary II, 7-9)

Mother of her own Creator!

What a marvelous woman, to be the mother of her own Creator! What an amazing distinction for a woman, to have a Son in common with God. The Father loves his Son; the Mother rejoices in her Son. The Father tells his Son: *From the womb, before the morning star, I begot you;* the Mother says to her same Son: From the womb, I, a virgin, brought you into the world.

She is amazed at her own glory, nor can she herself understand her elevation, for by the very fact of being made mother of the Creator she became with the best right mistress and queen of all creation. Truly, Mary, *he who is powerful did great things* for you; truly because he made you his own mother, *all the generations* of the ages *will call you blessed.*

RESPONSORY

How blessed are you, Virgin Mary,
for you carried within you the Lord, the Creator of the world.
— Mother of your Maker, you remain a virgin for ever.

Hail Mary, full of grace, the Lord is with you.
— Mother of your . . .

Or:

For our sake, the King of heaven chose to be born of his virgin mother,
to reclaim lost men for the heavenly kingdom.
—All the angels cry aloud with joy,
for God has come himself to save mankind.

Glory to God in the highest,
and peace to his people on earth.
—All the angels . . .

CANTICLE OF ZECHARIAH Luke 1:68-79

Ant. Blessed are you, Mary, because you believed that the Lord's words to you would be fulfilled.

The Messiah and his forerunner

Blessed be the Lord, the God of Israel;
he has come to his people and set them free.

He has raised up for us a mighty savior,
born of the house of his servant David.

Through his holy prophets he promised of old
that he would save us from our enemies,
from the hands of all who hate us.

He promised to show mercy to our fathers
and to remember his holy covenant.

This was the oath he swore to our father Abraham:
to set us free from the hands of our enemies,
free to worship him without fear,
holy and righteous in his sight
all the days of our life.

You, my child, shall be called the prophet of the Most High;
for you will go before the Lord to prepare his way,

to give his people knowledge of salvation
by the forgiveness of their sins.

In the tender compassion of our God
the dawn from on high shall break upon us,
to shine on those who dwell in darkness and the shadow of death,
and to guide our feet into the way of peace.

Glory to the Father, and to the Son, and to the Holy Spirit:

as it was in the beginning, is now, and will be for ever. Amen.

INTERCESSIONS

The Word of God existed before the creation of the universe yet was born among us in time. We praise and worship him as we cry out in joy:
Let the earth ring out with joy for you have come.

You are the eternal Word of God who flooded the world with joy at your birth,
— fill us with joy by the continuous gift of your life.

You saved us and by your birth revealed to us the covenant faithfulness of the Lord,
— help us to be faithful to the promises of our baptism.

You are the King of heaven and earth who sent messengers to announce peace to all,
— let our lives be filled with your peace.

You are the true vine that brings forth the fruit of life,
— make us branches of the vine, bearing much fruit.

Our Father . . .

CONCLUDING PRAYER

Father,
we are filled with the new light
by the coming of your Word among us.
May the light of faith
shine in our words and actions.

Grant this through our Lord Jesus Christ, your Son,
who lives and reigns with you and the Holy Spirit,
one God, for ever and ever.

Alternative Prayer

Almighty God and Father of light,
a child is born for us and a son is given to us.
Your eternal Word leaped down from heaven
in the silent watches of the night,
and now your church is filled with wonder

at the nearness of her God.
Open our hearts to receive his life
and increase our vision with the rising of dawn,
that our lives may be filled with his glory and his peace,
who lives and reigns for ever and ever.

May the Lord bless us,
protect us from evil
and bring us to everlasting life.
— Amen.

Evening Prayer

God, come to my assistance.
— Lord, make haste to help me.
Glory to the Father, and to the Son, and to the Holy Spirit:
as it was in the beginning, is now, and will be for ever. Amen.

HYMN

What child is this, who, laid to rest,
On Mary's lap is sleeping?
Whom angels greet with anthems sweet,
While shepherds watch are keeping?
This, this is Christ the King,
Whom shepherds guard and angels sing;
Haste, haste to bring him laud,
The Babe, the Son of Mary.

Why lies he in such mean estate,
Where ox and ass are feeding?
Good Christian, fear, for sinners here
The silent Word is pleading.
Nails, spear, shall pierce him through,
The cross be borne for me, for you:
Hail, hail, the Word made flesh,
The Babe, the Son of Mary!

So bring him incense, gold and myrrh,
Come, peasant, king, to own him;

The King of kings salvation brings,
Let loving hearts enthrone him.
Raise, raise the song on high,
The virgin sings her lullaby:
Joy, joy, for Christ is born,
The Babe, the Son of Mary!

Melody: Greensleeves 87.87.68.67
Music: 16th century English Melody
Text: William Chatterton Dix, 1837-1898

Or:

Rejoice, mother and heaven,
maiden and cloud, virgin and throne,
the boast and foundation of our Church.
Plead earnestly for us
that through you
we may obtain mercy on the Day of Judgment
and attain the good things reserved
for those who love God,
through the grace and love of our Lord Jesus Christ,
to whom with the Father and the Holy Spirit
be glory, power, and honor
now and for ever and for all eternity. Amen.

Saint John Chrysostom (344/354-407)

PSALMODY

Ant. 1 You have been endowed from your birth with princely gifts; in eternal splendor, before the dawn of light on earth, I have begotten you.

Or: Mary received a blessing from the Lord and loving kindness from God her savior.

Psalm 144

Prayer for victory and peace

Christ learned the art of warfare when he overcame the world, as he said: "I have overcome the world" (Saint Hilary).

I

Blessed be the Lord, my rock
who trains my arms for battle,
who prepares my hands for war.

He is my love, my fortress;
he is my stronghold, my savior,
my shield, my place of refuge.
He brings peoples under my rule.

Lord, what is man that you care for him,
mortal man, that you keep him in mind;
man, who is merely a breath,
whose life fades like a shadow?

Lower your heavens and come down;
touch the mountains; wreathe them in smoke.
Flash your lightnings; rout the foe,
shoot your arrows and put them to flight.

Reach down from heaven and save me;
draw me out from the mighty waters,
from the hands of alien foes
whose mouths are filled with lies,
whose hands are raised in perjury.

Ant. 2 With the Lord is unfailing love; great is his power to save.

Or: The Most High has made his dwelling place a holy temple.

II

To you, O God, will I sing a new song;
I will play on the ten-stringed harp
to you who give kings their victory,
who set David your servant free.

You set him free from the evil sword;
you rescued him from alien foes
whose mouths were filled with lies,
whose hands were raised in perjury.

Let our sons then flourish like saplings
grown tall and strong from their youth:
our daughters graceful as columns,
adorned as though for a palace.

Let our barns be filled to overflowing
with crops of every kind;
our sheep increasing by thousands,
myriads of sheep in our fields,
our cattle heavy with young,

no ruined wall, no exile,
no sound of weeping in our streets.
Happy the people with such blessings;
happy the people whose God is the Lord.

Ant. 3 In the beginning, before time began, the Word was God; today he is born, the Savior of the world.

Or: Glorious things are said of you, O Virgin Mary.

Canticle — Revelation 11:17-18; 12:10b-12a

The judgment of God

We praise you, the Lord God Almighty,
who is and who was.
You have assumed your great power,
you have begun your reign.

The nations have raged in anger,
but then came your day of wrath,
and the moment to judge the dead:
the time to reward your servants the prophets
and the holy ones who revere you,
the great and the small alike.

Now have salvation and power come,
the reign of our God and the authority
of his Anointed One.
For the accuser of our brothers is cast out,
who night and day accused them before God.

They defeated him by the blood of the Lamb
and by the word of their testimony;
love for life did not deter them from death.
So rejoice, you heavens,
and you that dwell therein!

First Reading — Galatians 4:4-5

When the fullness of time had come, God sent his Son, born of a woman, born under the law, to ransom those under the law, so that we might receive adoption.

Or — 1 John 3:1-8

See what love the Father has bestowed on us that we may be called the children of God. Yet so we are. The reason the world does not know us is that it did not know him. Beloved, we are God's children now; what we shall be has not yet been revealed. We do know that when it is revealed we shall be like him, for we shall see him as he is. Everyone who has this hope based on him makes himself pure, as he is pure.

Everyone who commits sin commits lawlessness, for sin is lawlessness. You know that he was revealed to take away sins, and in him there is no sin. No one who remains in him sins; no one who sins has seen him or known him. Children, let no one deceive you. The person who acts in righteousness is righteous, just as he is righteous. Whoever sins belongs to the devil, because the devil has sinned from the beginning. Indeed, the Son of God was revealed to destroy the works of the devil.

Second Reading

From a homily by Saint John Chrysostom, bishop
(Orientalia Christiana, vol. 32 [1966])

The birth of Mary's Son

Believe what we say about the Virgin, and do not hesitate to confess her to be both servant and Mother of God, both virgin and mother. She is a servant as the creature of him who was born of her; she is the Mother of God inasmuch as of her God was born in human flesh. She is a virgin because she did not conceive from the seed of man; she is a mother because she gave birth and became the mother of him who before all eternity was begotten of the Father.

She is therefore the mother of the Lord of angels and our mother; from her the Son of God received the human body in which he consented to be crucified. Do you desire to know how far the Virgin surpasses the powers of heaven? Give me your attention then. They veil their faces as they hover in fear and trembling, but she offers the human race to God, and through her we receive the forgiveness of our sins. She bore him whom the angels glorified when they came with reverence to be present at his birth. *Glory to God in the highest*, they sang, *and peace to his people on earth.*

Responsory

After the birth of your son, you remained a virgin.
— After the birth of your son, you remained a virgin.

Mother of God, intercede for us;
— you remained a virgin.

Glory to the Father . . .
— After the birth . . .

Or:

I shall glorify you, Lord, for you have rescued me.
— I shall glorify you, Lord, for you have rescued me.

You have not let my enemies rejoice over me.
— For you have rescued me.

Glory to the Father . . .
— I shall glorify . . .

Canticle of Mary — Luke 1:46-55

Ant. Christ the Lord is born today; today, the Savior has appeared. Earth echoes songs of angel choirs, archangels' joyful praise. Today on earth his friends exult: Glory to God in the highest.

My soul rejoices in the Lord

My soul proclaims the greatness of the Lord,
my spirit rejoices in God my Savior
for he has looked with favor on his lowly servant.

From this day all generations will call me blessed:
the Almighty has done great things for me,
and holy is his Name.

He has mercy on those who fear him
in every generation.

He has shown the strength of his arm,
he has scattered the proud in their conceit.

He has cast down the mighty from their thrones,
and has lifted up the lowly.

He has filled the hungry with good things,
and the rich he has sent away empty.

He has come to the help of his servant Israel
for he has remembered his promise of mercy,
the promise he made to our fathers,
to Abraham and his children for ever.

Glory to the Father, and to the Son, and to the Holy Spirit:
as it was in the beginning, is now, and will be for ever. Amen.

INTERCESSIONS

At the birth of Jesus, angels proclaimed peace to the world. We worship him now with joy, and we pray with hearts full of faith:
May your birth bring peace to all.

Lord, fill your holy people with whatever good they need,
—let the mystery of your birth be the source of our peace.

You came as chief shepherd and guardian of our lives,
—let the pope and bishops be faithful channels of your many gifts of grace.

King from all eternity, you desired to be born within time and to experience the day-to-day life of men and women,
—share your gift of unending life with us, weak people, doomed to death.

Awaited from the beginning of the world, you came only in the fullness of time,
— now reveal your presence to those who are still expecting you.

You became man and gave new life to our human condition in the grip of death,
—now give the fullness of life to all who have died.

Our Father . . .

Concluding Prayer

Lord God,
we praise you for creating man,
and still more for restoring him in Christ.
Your Son shared our weakness:
may we share his glory,
for he lives and reigns with you and the Holy Spirit,
one God, for ever and ever.

Alternative Prayer

God of love, Father of all,
the darkness that covered the earth
has given way to the bright dawn of your Word made flesh.
Make us a people of this light.
Make us faithful to your Word,
that we may bring your life to the waiting world.
Grant this through Christ our Lord.

May the Lord bless us,
protect us from evil
and bring us to everlasting life.
—Amen.

FRIDAY

Morning Prayer

God, come to my assistance.
— Lord, make haste to help me.

Glory to the Father, and to the Son, and to the Holy Spirit:
as it was in the beginning, is now, and will be for ever. Amen.

HYMN

The God whom earth and sea and sky
Adore and laud and magnify,
Whose might they own, whose praise they tell,
In Mary's body deigned to dwell.

O Mother blest! the chosen shrine
Wherein the Architect divine,
Whose hand contains the earth and sky,
Vouchsafed in hidden guise to lie:

Blest in the message Gabriel brought;
Blest in the work the Spirit wrought;
Most blest, to bring to human birth
The long desired of all the earth.

O Lord, the Virgin born, to thee
Eternal praise and glory be,
Whom with the Father we adore
And Holy Ghost for ever more.

Melody: Eisenach L.M.

Music: Johan H. Schein, 1586-1630
Text: Venantius Fortunatus 530-609
Translator: J.M. Neale, 1818-1866

Or:

Virgin of virgins,
I choose you today
as my sovereign, my queen, my empress,
and I declare myself, as I am in fact,
your servant and your slave.

I invoke your royal name of Mary,
that is, sovereign Lady,
and beg of you with all my heart
to admit me into the privileged circle
of your family
as one of your servants,
to do your will
as a humble slave and a loving child.

As a sign of your acceptance
engrave on my heart
with the fire of your love,
not the brand of an unwilling slave,
but those two gracious words of the angel:
Ave Maria.

As long as I draw breath
may your burning love ensure
that I bear these words
in my heart and in my memory,
and that until my dying breath
my will may be always on fire
with my great desire to serve you,
my sovereign and my queen,
glorious in your majesty.

Though I am in every way unworthy
of so honorable a title,
I resolve sincerely to be your slave,
to serve you wholeheartedly,
to protect your name,
and that of your Son,
against every insult,
as far as it may rest with me,
and never to allow anyone in my charge
to offend your Son in any way.

By your tender love for your Son,
by the glories you have received
from the Most Holy Trinity,

do not reject me from your service
but as my sovereign and my queen
preside over all my actions,
command whatever you will,
direct all my work,
remedy all its defects.

During my whole life
rule over me
as your servant and slave.
At the hour of my death,
as I hope for
at the end of my loving servitude
among the privileged members of your family,
receive my soul
and escort it
into the presence of God.

Bartolomé de Los Ríos (1580-1652)

Psalmody

Ant. 1 My soul clings to you, Lord Jesus Christ.

Or: Mary gave birth to Jesus, who is called the Christ.

Psalm 51

O God, have mercy on me

Your inmost being must be renewed, and you must put on the new man (Ephesians 4:23-24).

Have mercy on me, God, in your kindness.
In your compassion blot out my offense.
O wash me more and more from my guilt
and cleanse me from my sin.

My offenses truly I know them;
my sin is always before me.
Against you, you alone, have I sinned;
what is evil in your sight I have done.

That you may be justified when you give sentence
and be without reproach when you judge.
O see, in guilt I was born,
a sinner was I conceived.

Indeed you love truth in the heart;
then in the secret of my heart teach me wisdom.
O purify me, then I shall be clean;
O wash me, I shall be whiter than snow.

Make me hear rejoicing and gladness,
that the bones you have crushed may revive.
From my sins turn away your face
and blot out all my guilt.

A pure heart create for me, O God,
put a steadfast spirit within me.
Do not cast me away from your presence,
nor deprive me of your holy spirit.

Give me again the joy of your help;
with a spirit of fervor sustain me,
that I may teach transgressors your ways
and sinners may return to you.

O rescue me, God, my helper,
and my tongue shall ring out your goodness.
O Lord, open my lips
and my mouth shall declare your praise.

For in sacrifice you take no delight,
burnt offering from me you would refuse,
my sacrifice, a contrite spirit.
A humbled, contrite heart you will not spurn.

In your goodness, show favor to Zion;
rebuild the walls of Jerusalem.
Then you will be pleased with lawful sacrifice,
holocausts offered on your altar.

Ant. 2 Let us rejoice that we have been made sharers
in Christ's passion.

Or: Holy Mother, on the cross Christ entrusted us to you as your children. Today we join with you in praising him.

Canticle Tobit 13:8-11, 13-15

Thanksgiving for the people's deliverance

He showed me the holy city Jerusalem which shone with the glory of God (Revelation 21:10-11).

Let all men speak of the Lord's majesty,
and sing his praises in Jerusalem.

O Jerusalem, holy city,
he scourged you for the works of your hands,
but will again pity the children of the righteous.

Praise the Lord for his goodness,
and bless the King of the ages,
so that his tent may be rebuilt in you with joy.

May he gladden within you all who were captives;
all who were ravaged may he cherish within you
for all generations to come.

A bright light will shine to all parts of the earth;
many nations shall come to you from afar,
and the inhabitants of all the limits of the earth,
drawn to you by the name of the Lord God,
bearing in their hands their gifts for the King of heaven.

Every generation shall give joyful praise in you,
and shall call you the chosen one,
through all ages forever.

Go, then, rejoice over the children of the righteous,
who shall be gathered together
and shall bless the Lord of the ages.

Happy are those who love you,
and happy those who rejoice in your prosperity.

Happy are all the men who shall grieve over you,
over all your chastisements,

for they shall rejoice in you
as they behold all your joy forever.

My spirit blesses the Lord, the great King.

Ant. 3 It has pleased the Father to reconcile all creation in himself through the blood of Christ.

Or: The Virgin Mary, crowned with a diadem of twelve stars, is exalted above the choirs of angels.

Psalm 147:12-20

The restoration of Jerusalem

Come, I will show you the bride of the Lamb (Revelation 21:9).

O praise the Lord, Jerusalem!
Zion, praise your God!

He has strengthened the bars of your gates,
he has blessed the children within you.
He established peace on your borders,
he feeds you with finest wheat.

He sends out his word to the earth
and swiftly runs his command.
He showers down snow white as wool,
he scatters hoar-frost like ashes.

He hurls down hailstones like crumbs.
The waters are frozen at his touch;
he sends forth his word and it melts them:
at the breath of his mouth the waters flow.

He makes his word known to Jacob,
to Israel his laws and decrees.
He has not dealt thus with other nations;
he has not taught them his decrees.

FIRST READING Colossians 1:24-25

Now I rejoice in my sufferings for your sake, and in my flesh I am filling up what is lacking in the afflictions of Christ on behalf of his body, which is the church, of which I am a minister in accordance with God's stewardship given to me to bring to completion for you the word of God.

Or Proverbs 8:32-35; 9:1-6, 10-12

"So now, O children, listen to me;
instruction and wisdom do not reject!
Happy the man who obeys me,
and happy those who keep my ways,
Happy the man watching daily at my gates,
waiting at my doorposts;
For he who finds me finds life,
and wins favor from the Lord;
But he who misses me harms himself;
all who hate me love death."

Wisdom has built her house,
she has set up her seven columns;
She has dressed her meat, mixed her wine,
yes, she has spread her table.
She has sent out her maidens; she calls
from the heights out over the city:

"Let whoever is simple turn in here;
to him who lacks understanding, I say,
Come, eat of my food,
and drink of the wine I have mixed!
Forsake foolishness that you may live;
advance in the way of understanding.
For by me your days will be multiplied
and the years of your life increased."

The beginning of wisdom is the fear of the Lord,
and knowledge of the Holy One is understanding.
If you are wise, it is to your own advantage;
and if you are arrogant, you alone shall bear it.

Second Reading

From a sermon by Saint Lawrence Justinian, bishop

(Sermo 8, in festo Purificationis B.M.V.: Opera, 2 Venetiis 1751, 38-39)

Mary stored up all these things in her heart

While Mary contemplated all she had come to know through reading, listening and observing, she grew in faith, increased in merits, and was more illuminated by wisdom and more consumed by the fire of charity. The heavenly mysteries were opened to her, and she was filled with joy; she became fruitful by the Spirit, was being directed toward God, and watched over protectively while on earth.

So remarkable are the divine graces that they elevate one from the lowest depths to the highest summit, and transform one to a greater holiness. How entirely blessed was the mind of the Virgin which, through the indwelling and guidance of the Spirit, was always and in every way open to the power of the Word of God. She was not led by her own senses, nor by her own will; thus she accomplished outwardly through her body what wisdom from within gave to her faith.

It was fitting for divine Wisdom, which created itself a home in the Church, to use the intervention of the most blessed Mary in guarding the law, purifying the mind, giving an example of humility and providing a spiritual sacrifice.

Imitate her, O faithful soul. Enter into the deep recesses of your heart so that you may be purified spiritually and cleansed from your sins. God places more value on good will in all we do than on the works themselves.

Therefore, whether we give ourselves to God in the work of contemplation or whether we serve the needs of our neighbor by good works, we accomplish these things because the love of Christ urges us on. The acceptable offering of the spiritual purification is accomplished not in a man-made temple but in the recesses of the heart where the Lord Jesus freely enters.

RESPONSORY

Through you we drink from the wellsprings of salvation, O Blessed Virgin Mary.
— Through you we drink from the wellsprings of salvation, O Blessed Virgin Mary.

From the sacred wounds of Christ,
— O Blessed Virgin Mary.

Glory to the Father . . .
— Through you we . . .

Or:

O Virgin Mary, no other daughter of Jerusalem is your equal,
for you are the mother of the King of kings,
you are the Queen of heaven and of angels.
— Blessed are you among women,
and blessed is the fruit of your womb.

Hail, full of grace; the Lord is with you.
— Blessed are you . . .

CANTICLE OF ZECHARIAH Luke 1:68-79

Ant. Rejoice, O sorrowful Mother; after your great sufferings, you shine forth as Queen, enthroned beside your Son.

The Messiah and his forerunner

Blessed be the Lord, the God of Israel;
he has come to his people and set them free.

He has raised up for us a mighty savior,
born of the house of his servant David.

Through his holy prophets he promised of old
that he would save us from our enemies,
from the hands of all who hate us.

He promised to show mercy to our fathers
and to remember his holy covenant.

This was the oath he swore to our father Abraham:
to set us free from the hands of our enemies,
free to worship him without fear,
holy and righteous in his sight
all the days of our life.

You, my child, shall be called the prophet of the Most High;
for you will go before the Lord to prepare his way,

to give his people knowledge of salvation
by the forgiveness of their sins.

In the tender compassion of our God
the dawn from on high shall break upon us,
to shine on those who dwell in darkness and the shadow of death,
and to guide our feet into the way of peace.

Glory to the Father, and to the Son, and to the Holy Spirit:
as it was in the beginning, is now, and will be for ever. Amen.

INTERCESSIONS

Let us glorify our Savior, who chose the Virgin Mary for his mother. Let us ask him:
May your mother intercede for us, Lord.

Sun of Justice, the immaculate Virgin was the white dawn announcing your rising,
— grant that we may always live in the light of your coming.

Eternal Word, you chose Mary as the uncorrupted ark of your dwelling place,
— free us from the corruption of sin.

Savior of mankind, your mother stood at the foot of your cross,
— grant, through her intercession, that we may rejoice to share in your passion.

With ultimate generosity and love, you gave Mary as a mother to your beloved disciple,
— help us to live as worthy sons of so noble a mother.

Our Father . . .

Concluding Prayer

Father,
as your Son was raised on the cross,
his mother Mary stood by him, sharing his sufferings.
May your Church be united with Christ
in his suffering and death
and so come to share in his rising to new life,
where he lives and reigns with you and the Holy Spirit,
one God, for ever and ever.

May the Lord bless us,
protect us from all evil
and bring us to everlasting life.
—Amen.

Evening Prayer

God, come to my assistance.
— Lord, make haste to help me.
Glory to the Father, and to the Son, and to the Holy Spirit:
as it was in the beginning, is now, and will be for ever. Amen.

Hymn

Ye who own the faith of Jesus,
Sing the wonders that were done,
When the love of God the Father
O'er our sin the victory won,
When he made the Virgin Mary
Mother of his only Son.
Hail, Mary, full of grace.

Blessed were the chosen people
Out of whom the Lord did come,

Blessed was the land of promise
Fashioned for his earthly home;
But more blessed for the mother,
She who bore him in her womb.
Hail, Mary, full of grace.

Wherefore let all faithful people
Tell the honor of her name,
Let the Church in her foreshadowed
Part in her thanksgiving claim;
What Christ's mother sang in gladness
Let Christ's people sing the same.
Hail, Mary, full of grace.

Praise, O Mary, praise the Father,
Praise thy Savior and thy Son,
Praise the everlasting Spirit,
Who hath made thee ark and throne.
O'er all creatures high exalted,
Lowly praise the three in one.
Hail, Mary, full of grace.

Melody: Den das Vaters Sinn geboren 87.87.876

Music: J.A. Freylinghausen, 1670-1739
Text: V.S.S. Coles, 1845-1929

Or:

The Spirit spread his wings over the Virgin's womb.
She conceived and gave birth.
And she became a virginal mother by great mercy.
She conceived and gave birth to a son without pain,
and there was a purpose for this.
She did not ask for a midwife to aid her,
because God saw to her delivery.
Like a human being, she gave birth according to the will of God.
Manifestly she gave birth.
With great power she acquired him.

With thanksgiving she loved him.
With kindness she guarded him.
With grandeur she manifested him.
Alleluia!

Odes of Solomon (2nd century) 19, 6-11

PSALMODY

Ant. 1 Through his cross, Christ our peace has reconciled us to God.

Or: The angel Gabriel brought God's message to Mary, and she conceived by the power of the Holy Spirit.

Psalm 145

Praise of God's majesty

Lord, you are the Just One, who was and who is (Revelation 16:5).

I

I will give you glory, O God my King,
I will bless your name for ever.

I will bless you day after day
and praise your name for ever.
The Lord is great, highly to be praised,
his greatness cannot be measured.

Age to age shall proclaim your works,
shall declare your mighty deeds,
shall speak of your splendor and glory,
tell the tale of your wonderful works.

They will speak of your terrible deeds,
recount your greatness and might.
They will recall your abundant goodness;
age to age shall ring out your justice.

The Lord is kind and full of compassion,
slow to anger, abounding in love.
How good is the Lord to all,
compassionate to all his creatures.

All your creatures shall thank you, O Lord,
and your friends shall repeat their blessing.
They shall speak of the glory of your reign
and declare your might, O God,

to make known to men your mighty deeds
and the glorious splendor of your reign.
Yours is an everlasting kingdom;
your rule lasts from age to age.

Ant. 2 We have come to the city of the living God, and to Jesus, mediator of the new Covenant.

Or: His mother stood beside the cross.

II

The Lord is faithful in all his words
and loving in all his deeds.
The Lord supports all who fall
and raises all who are bowed down.

The eyes of all creatures look to you
and you give them their food in due time.
You open wide your hand,
grant the desires of all who live.

The Lord is just in all his ways
and loving in all his deeds.
He is close to all who call him,
who call on him from their hearts.

He grants the desires of those who fear him,
he hears their cry and he saves them.
The Lord protects all who love him;
but the wicked he will utterly destroy.

Let me speak the praise of the Lord,
let all mankind bless his holy name
for ever, for ages unending.

Ant. 3 In Christ we have redemption through his blood.

Or: Rejoice, O Virgin Mother; Christ has risen from the dead.

Canticle Revelation 15:3-4

Hymn of adoration

Mighty and wonderful are your works,
Lord God Almighty!
Righteous and true are your ways,
O King of the nations!

Who would dare refuse you honor,
or the glory due your name, O Lord?

Since you alone are holy,
all nations shall come
and worship in your presence.
Your mighty deeds are clearly seen.

FIRST READING 2 Timothy 2:10-12a

I bear with everything for the sake of those who are chosen, so that they too may obtain the salvation that is in Christ Jesus, together with eternal glory. This saying is trustworthy:

If we have died with him
we shall also live with him;
if we persevere
we shall also reign with him.

Or 2 John 4-13

I rejoiced greatly to find some of your children walking in the truth just as we were commanded by the Father. But now, Lady, I ask you, not as though I were writing a new commandment but the one we have had from the beginning: let us love one another. For this is love, that we walk according to his commandments; this is the commandment, as you heard from the beginning, in which you should walk.

Many deceivers have gone out into the world, those who do not acknowledge Jesus Christ as coming in the flesh; such is the deceitful one and the antichrist. Look to yourselves that you do not lose what we worked for but may receive a full recompense. Anyone who is so "progressive" as not to remain in the teaching of the Christ does not have God; whoever remains in the teaching has the Father and the Son. If anyone comes to you and does not bring this doctrine, do not receive him in your house or even greet him; for whoever greets him shares in his evil works.

Although I have much to write to you, I do not intend to use paper and ink. Instead, I hope to visit you and to speak face to face so that our joy may be complete. The children of your chosen sister send you greetings.

Second Reading

From a sermon by Saint Bernard, abbot

(Sermo in dom. infra oct. Assumptionis, 14-15: Opera omnia, Edit. Cisterc. 5 [1968], 273-274)

His mother stood by the cross

The martyrdom of the Virgin is set forth both in the prophecy of Simeon and in the actual story of our Lord's passion. The holy man said of the infant Jesus: *He has been established as a sign which will be contradicted.* He went on to say to Mary: *And your own heart will be pierced by a sword.*

Truly, O blessed Mother, a sword has pierced your heart. For only by passing through your heart could the sword enter the flesh of your Son. Indeed, after your Jesus—who belongs to everyone, but is especially yours—gave up his life, the cruel spear, which was not withheld from his lifeless body, tore open his side. Clearly it did not touch his soul and could not harm him, but it did pierce your heart. For surely his soul was no longer there, but yours could not be torn away. Thus the violence of sorrow has cut through your heart, and we rightly call you more than martyr, since the effect of compassion in you has gone beyond the endurance of physical suffering.

Or were those words: *Woman, behold your Son,* not more than a sword to you, truly piercing your heart, cutting through to the division between soul and spirit? What an exchange! John is given to you in place of Jesus, the servant in place of the Lord, the disciple in place of the master; the son of Zebedee replaces the Son of God, a mere man replaces God himself. How could these words not pierce your most loving heart, when the mere remembrance of them breaks ours, hearts of stone and iron though they are!

Or:

From a sermon by Saint Bernard, abbot

(Sermo in dom. infra oct. Assumptionis, 14-15: Opera omnia, Edit. Cisterc. 5 [1968],273-274)

A martyr in spirit

Do not be surprised, brothers, that Mary is said to be a martyr in spirit. Let him be surprised who does not remember the words of Paul, that one of the greatest crimes of the Gentiles was that they were without love. That was far from the heart of Mary; let it be far from her servants.

Perhaps someone will say: "Had she not known before that he would die?" Undoubtedly. "Did she not expect him to rise again at once?" Surely. "And still she grieved over her crucified Son?" Intensely.

Who are you and what is the source of your wisdom that you are more surprised at the compassion of Mary than at the passion of Mary's Son? For if he could die in body, could she not die with him in spirit? He died in body through a love greater than anyone had known. She died in spirit through a love unlike any other since his.

Responsory

Holy Mary, heaven's Queen and our Lady, you stood by the cross of the Lord.
— Holy Mary, heaven's Queen and our Lady, you stood by the cross of the Lord.

Happy is she, who without dying has won the martyr's crown.
— You stood by the cross of the Lord.

Glory to the Father . . .
— Holy Mary, heaven's . . .

Or:

The Lord has chosen her,
his loved one from the beginning.
— The Lord has chosen her,
his loved one from the beginning.

He has taken her to live with him,
— his loved one from the beginning.

Glory to the Father . . .
— The Lord has . . .

Canticle of Mary — Luke 1:46-55

Ant. When Jesus saw his mother standing beside the cross with the disciple whom he loved, he said to her: Woman, behold your son. Then he said to the disciple: Behold your mother.

My soul rejoices in the Lord

My soul proclaims the greatness of the Lord,
my spirit rejoices in God my Savior
for he has looked with favor on his lowly servant.

From this day all generations will call me blessed:
the Almighty has done great things for me,
and holy is his Name.

He has mercy on those who fear him
in every generation.

He has shown the strength of his arm,
he has scattered the proud in their conceit.

He has cast down the mighty from their thrones,
and has lifted up the lowly.

He has filled the hungry with good things,
and the rich he has sent away empty.

He has come to the help of his servant Israel
for he has remembered his promise of mercy,
the promise he made to our fathers,
to Abraham and his children for ever.

Glory to the Father, and to the Son, and to the Holy Spirit:
as it was in the beginning, is now, and will be for ever. Amen.

Intercessions

Let us praise God our almighty Father, who wished that Mary, his Son's mother, be celebrated by each generation. Now in need we ask:
Mary, full of grace, intercede for us.

O God, worker of miracles, you made the Immaculate Virgin Mary share body and soul in your Son's glory in heaven,
— direct the hearts of your children to that same glory.

You made Mary our mother. Through her intercession grant strength to the weak, comfort to the sorrowing, pardon to sinners,
— salvation and peace to all.

You made Mary full of grace,
— grant all men the joyful abundance of your grace.

Make your Church of one mind and one heart in love,
— and help all those who believe to be one in prayer with Mary, the mother of Jesus.

You crowned Mary queen of heaven,
— may all the dead rejoice in your kingdom with the saints for ever.

Our Father . . .

Concluding Prayer

Father,
as your Son was raised on the cross,
his mother Mary stood by him, sharing his sufferings.
May your Church be united with Christ
in his suffering and death
and so come to share in his rising to new life,
where he lives and reigns with you and the Holy Spirit,
one God, for ever and ever.

May the Lord bless us,
protect us from all evil
and bring us to everlasting life.
— Amen.

SATURDAY

Morning Prayer

God, come to my assistance.
— Lord, make haste to help me.
Glory to the Father, and to the Son, and to the Holy Spirit:
as it was in the beginning, is now, and will be for ever. Amen.

HYMN

Hail, holy Queen of the Heavens.
Hail, holy Queen of the Angels.
Hail, Root of Jesse.
Hail, Gate of Heaven.
By you the Light has entered the world.
Rejoice, glorious Virgin,

Beautiful among all women.
Hail, radiant Splendor,
Intercede with Christ for us.

Melody: Hail, Holy Queen

Music: Lucien Deiss, C.S.Sp., 1965
Text: Lucien Deiss, C.S.Sp., 1965

Or:

Holy Mary,
my Queen and sovereign Lady,
I give you myself,
trusting in your fidelity and your protection.

I surrender myself entirely
to your motherly tenderness,
my body, my soul,
all that I am, all that I possess,
for the whole of this day,
for every moment of my life,
and especially at the hour of my death.

I entrust to you once more
all my hopes, all my consolations,
all my anxieties, all my troubles,
my life, my dying breath,
so that by your prayers and merits,
I may have, in all I do, one only goal,
your good pleasure and the holy will of your Son.

Père Raphael (17th century)

PSALMODY

Ant. 1 Blessed are you, O Mary, for the world's salvation came forth through you; now in glory, you rejoice for ever with the Lord.

Or: Arise, O Virgin Queen, you are for ever worthy of our praise; take your place in the glorious dwelling place of the eternal King.

Psalm 92

Praise of God the creator

Sing in praise of Christ's redeeming work (Saint Athanasius).

It is good to give thanks to the Lord,
to make music to your name, O Most High,
to proclaim your love in the morning
and your truth in the watches of the night,
on the ten-stringed lyre and the lute,
with the murmuring sound of the harp.

Your deeds, O Lord, have made me glad;
for the work of your hands I shout with joy.
O Lord, how great are your works!
How deep are your designs!
The foolish man cannot know this
and the fool cannot understand.

Though the wicked spring up like grass
and all who do evil thrive:
they are doomed to be eternally destroyed.—

But you, Lord, are eternally on high.
See how your enemies perish;
all doers of evil are scattered.

To me you give the wild-ox's strength;
you anoint me with the purest oil.
My eyes looked in triumph on my foes;
my ears heard gladly of their fall.
The just will flourish like the palm-tree
and grow like a Lebanon cedar.

Planted in the house of the Lord,
they will flourish in the courts of our God,
still bearing fruit when they are old,
still full of sap, still green,
to proclaim that the Lord is just.
In him, my rock, there is no wrong.

Ant. 2 The Virgin Mary is exalted above the choirs of angels; let all believers rejoice and bless the Lord.

Or: The Lord has chosen her, his loved one from the beginning. He has taken her to live with him.

Canticle Ezekiel 36:24-28

The Lord will renew his people

They will be his own people, and God himself will be with them, their own God (Revelation 21:3).

I will take you away from among the nations,
gather you from all the foreign lands,
and bring you back to your own land.

I will sprinkle clean water upon you
to cleanse you from all your impurities,
and from all your idols I will cleanse you.

I will give you a new heart
and place a new spirit within you,
taking from your bodies your stony hearts
and giving you natural hearts.

I will put my spirit within you,
and make you live by my statutes,
careful to observe my decrees.

You shall live in the land I gave your fathers;
you shall be my people,
and I will be your God.

Ant. 3 The Lord has made you so glorious that your praise will never cease to resound among men.

Or: Glorious things are said of you, O Virgin Mary.

Psalm 8

The majesty of the Lord and man's dignity

The Father gave Christ lordship of creation and made him head of the Church (Ephesians 1:22).

How great is your name, O Lord our God,
through all the earth!

Your majesty is praised above the heavens;
on the lips of children and babes
you have found praise to foil your enemy,
to silence the foe and the rebel.

When I see the heavens, the work of your hands,
the moon and the stars which you arranged,
what is man that you should keep him in mind,
mortal man that you care for him?

Yet you have made him little less than a god;
with glory and honor you crowned him,
gave him power over the works of your hand,
put all things under his feet.

All of them, sheep and cattle,
yes, even the savage beasts,
birds of the air, and fish
that make their way through the waters.

How great is your name, O Lord our God,
through all the earth!

FIRST READING See Isaiah 61:10

I rejoice heartily in the Lord,
in my God is the joy of my soul;
For he has clothed me with a robe of salvation,
and wrapped me in a mantle of justice,
like a bride bedecked with her jewels.

Or Revelation 12:1

A great sign appeared in the sky, a woman clothed with the sun, with the moon under her feet, and on her head a crown of twelve stars.

Or Judith 13:17-20

All the people were greatly astonished. They bowed down and worshiped God, saying with one accord, "Blessed are you, our God, who today have brought to nought the enemies of your people."

Then Uzziah said to her: "Blessed are you, daughter, by the Most High God, above all the women on earth; and blessed be the Lord God, the creator of heaven and earth, who guided your blow at the head of the chief of our enemies. Your deed of hope will never be forgotten by those who tell of the might of God.

"May God make this redound to your everlasting honor, rewarding you with blessings, because you risked your life when your people were being oppressed, and you averted our disaster, walking uprightly before our God." And all the people answered, "Amen! Amen!"

SECOND READING

From a letter from Paschasius Radbert, abbot

(Letter *Cogitis me* 20-23, 26-28: PL 30, 122-42)

Mary is taken from earth

Today the glorious, ever-virgin Mary ascends to heaven. I urge you to rejoice, for, if I may so put it, she has been raised up in an ineffable way to be with Christ who reigns for ever. The Queen of the world is today taken from the earth and from this present evil time. I say again: rejoice, because she who is sure of her imperishable glory has reached the palace of heaven.

Exult, I say, and rejoice, and let the whole world rejoice, because this day Salvation has drawn nearer for us all. . . .

"Hail, Mary, full of grace; the Lord is with you; blessed are you among women." It was fitting that the Virgin should be given such gifts and be full of grace, since she has bestowed glory on heaven and has brought God and peace to the earth, faith to pagans, an end to vice, order to life, and discipline to morals.

And it was right that an angel be sent to the Virgin, because virginity always means kinship with the angels. . . .

"Rejoice," the angel says, "for you are full of grace." Yes, full! for while a share of grace was given to others, the undiminished fullness of grace was poured into Mary.

Responsory

The Virgin Mary was taken up to heaven.
— The Virgin Mary was taken up to heaven.

For all eternity she shares the victory of Christ.
— The Virgin Mary was taken up to heaven.

Glory to the Father . . .
— The Virgin . . .

Or:

After the birth of your son, you remained a virgin.
— After the birth of your son, you remained a virgin.

Mother of God, intercede for us;
— you remained a virgin,

Glory to the Father . . .
— After the birth of your son, you remained a virgin.

CANTICLE OF ZECHARIAH Luke 1:68-79

Ant. This daughter of Jerusalem is lovely and beautiful as she ascends to heaven like the rising sun at daybreak.

The Messiah and his forerunner

Blessed be the Lord, the God of Israel;
he has come to his people and set them free.

He has raised up for us a mighty savior,
born of the house of his servant David.

Through his holy prophets he promised of old
that he would save us from our enemies,
from the hands of all who hate us.

He promised to show mercy to our fathers
and to remember his holy covenant.

This was the oath he swore to our father Abraham:
to set us free from the hands of our enemies,
free to worship him without fear,
holy and righteous in his sight
all the days of our life.

You, my child, shall be called the prophet of the Most High;
for you will go before the Lord to prepare his way,

to give his people knowledge of salvation
by the forgiveness of their sins.

In the tender compassion of our God
the dawn from on high shall break upon us,
to shine on those who dwell in darkness and the shadow of death,
and to guide our feet into the way of peace.

Glory to the Father, and to the Son, and to the Holy Spirit:
as it was in the beginning, is now, and will be for ever. Amen.

INTERCESSIONS

Let us glorify our Savior, who chose the Virgin Mary for his mother. Let us ask him:
May your mother intercede for us, Lord.

Eternal Word, you chose Mary as the uncorrupted ark of your dwelling place,
— free us from the corruption of sin.

You are our redeemer, who made the immaculate Virgin Mary your purest home and the sanctuary of the Holy Spirit,
— make us temples of your Spirit for ever.

King of kings, you lifted up your mother, body and soul, into heaven,
— help us to fix our thoughts on things above.

Lord of heaven and earth, you crowned Mary and set her at your right hand as queen,
— make us worthy to share this glory.

Our Father . . .

CONCLUDING PRAYER

All-powerful and ever-living God,
you raised the sinless Virgin Mary,
mother of your Son,
body and soul to the glory of heaven.
May we see heaven as our final goal
and come to share her glory.

We ask this through our Lord Jesus Christ, your Son,
who lives and reigns with you and the Holy Spirit,
one God, for ever and ever.

May the Lord bless us,
protect us from all evil
and bring us to everlasting life.
—Amen.

Evening Prayer

God, come to my assistance.
— Lord, make haste to help me.
Glory to the Father, and to the Son, and to the Holy Spirit:
as it was in the beginning, is now, and will be for ever. Amen.

Hymn

Praise to Mary, Heaven's Gate,
Guiding Star of Christians' way,
Mother of our Lord and King,
Light and hope to souls astray.

When you heard the call of God
Choosing to fulfill his plan,
By your perfect act of love
Hope was born in fallen man.

Help us to amend our ways,
Halt the devil's strong attack,
Walk with us the narrow path,
Beg for us the grace we lack.

Mary, show your motherhood,
Bring your children's prayers to Christ,
Christ, your son, who ransomed man,
Who, for us, was sacrificed.

Virgin chosen, singly blest,
Ever faithful to God's call,
Guide us in this earthly life,
Guard us lest, deceived, we fall.

Mary, help us live our faith
So that we may see your son;
Join our humble prayers to yours,
Till life's ceaseless war is won.

Praise the Father, praise the Son,
Praise the holy Paraclete;

Offer all through Mary's hands,
Let her make our prayers complete.

Melody: Gott sei dank 77.77 — Music: Freylinghausen's *Gesangbuch,* 1704
Text: *Ave Maris Stella,* 9th century
Translator: Rev. M. Quinn, O.P. et al., alt.

Or:

My Lady,
my refuge, life, and help,
my armor and my boast,
my hope and my strength,
grant that I may enjoy
the ineffable, inconceivable gifts of your Son,
your God and our God,
in the heavenly kingdom.
For I know surely
that you have power to do as you will,
since you are Mother of the Most High.
Therefore, Lady Most Pure,
I beg you
that I may not be disappointed in my expectations
but may obtain them, O spouse of God,
who bore him who is the expectation of all:
Our Lord Jesus Christ,
true God and Master of all things,
visible and invisible,
to whom belongs all glory, honor, and respect,
now and always and through endless ages. Amen.

Saint Germanus of Constantinople (c. 634-730)

Psalmody

Ant. 1 Mary has been taken up to heaven; the angels rejoice. They bless the Lord and sing his praises.

Or: Christ ascended into heaven and prepared an everlasting place for his immaculate Mother.

Psalm 122

Holy city Jerusalem

You have come to Mount Zion, to the city of the living God, heavenly Jerusalem (Hebrews 12:22).

I rejoiced when I heard them say:
"Let us go to God's house."
And now our feet are standing
within your gates, O Jerusalem.

Jerusalem is built as a city
strongly compact.
It is there that the tribes go up,
the tribes of the Lord.

For Israel's law it is,
there to praise the Lord's name.
There were set the thrones of judgment
of the house of David.

For the peace of Jerusalem pray:
"Peace be to your homes!
May peace reign in your walls,
in your palaces, peace!"

For love of my brethren and friends
I say: "Peace upon you!"
For love of the house of the Lord
I will ask for your good.

Ant. 2 The Virgin Mary was taken up to the heavenly bridal chamber where the King of kings is seated on a starry throne.

Or: Through Eve the gates of heaven were closed to all mankind; through the Virgin Mother they were opened wide again.

Psalm 130

A cry from the depths

He himself will save his people from their sins (Matthew 1:21).

Out of the depths I cry to you, O Lord,
Lord, hear my voice!
O let your ears be attentive
to the voice of my pleading.

If you, O Lord, should mark our guilt,
Lord, who would survive?
But with you is found forgiveness:
for this we revere you.

My soul is waiting for the Lord,
I count on his word.
My soul is longing for the Lord
more than watchman for daybreak.
Let the watchman count on daybreak
and Israel on the Lord.

Because with the Lord there is mercy
and fullness of redemption,
Israel indeed he will redeem
from all its iniquity.

Ant. 3 We share the fruit of life through you, O daughter blessed by the Lord.

Or: The Virgin Mary has been exalted above all the heavens; come, let all men glorify Christ the King, whose kingdom will endure for ever.

Canticle Philippians 2:6-11

Christ, God's holy servant

Though he was in the form of God,
Jesus did not deem equality with God
something to be grasped at.

Rather, he emptied himself
and took the form of a slave,
being born in the likeness of men.

He was known to be of human estate,
and it was thus that he humbled himself,
obediently accepting even death,
death on a cross!

Because of this,
God highly exalted him
and bestowed on him the name
above every other name,

So that at Jesus' name
every knee must bend
in the heavens, on the earth,
and under the earth,
and every tongue proclaim
to the glory of God the Father:
JESUS CHRIST IS LORD!

FIRST READING — 1 Corinthians 15:22-23

Just as in Adam all die, so too in Christ shall all be brought to life, but each one in proper order: Christ the firstfruits; then, at his coming, those who belong to Christ.

Or — Judith 13:17b, 18a

Blessed are you, our God, who today have brought to nought the enemies of your people. Blessed are you, daughter, by the Most High God, above all the women on earth.

Or — Revelation 12:1

A great sign appeared in the sky, a woman clothed with the sun, with the moon under her feet, and on her head a crown of twelve stars.

Or Romans 5:12-21

Just as through one person sin entered the world, and through sin, death, and thus death came to all, inasmuch as all sinned for up to the time of the law, sin was in the world, though sin is not accounted when there is no law. But death reigned from Adam to Moses, even over those who did not sin after the pattern of the trespass of Adam, who is the type of the one who was to come.

But the gift is not like the transgression. For if by that one person's transgression the many died, how much more did the grace of God and the gracious gift of the one person Jesus Christ overflow for the many. And the gift is not like the result of the one person's sinning. For after one sin there was the judgment that brought condemnation; but the gift, after many transgressions, brought acquittal. For if, by the transgression of one person, death came to reign through that one, how much more will those who receive the abundance of grace and of the gift of justification come to reign in life through the one person Jesus Christ. In conclusion, just as through one transgression condemnation came upon all, so through one righteous act acquittal and life came to all. For just as through the disobedience of one person the many were made sinners, so through the obedience of one the many will be made righteous. The law entered in so that transgression might increase but, where sin increased, grace overflowed all the more, so that, as sin reigned in death, grace also might reign through justification for eternal life through Jesus Christ our Lord.

Second Reading

From a homily on the falling asleep of the Blessed Virgin Mary by Saint Germanus of Constantinople, bishop

(In Dormitionem B. Mariae I: PG 98, 345-348).

The Assumption of Mary

Truly, yes truly, and again I shall say in thanksgiving: even though you have left us, you have not deserted the Christian race. You who are like incorruptible life have not abandoned our mortal world, but on the contrary you draw near to those who call upon your name. You are found by those who faithfully seek you. And these visions indicate a living and continually active spirit and an everlasting body. For how could dissolution of the body return you to dust and ashes, you who delivered the human race from the destruction of death through the incarnation of your Son?

Indeed you left our earth to prove that the mystery of the awe-inspiring incarnation was really fulfilled. The fact that you waited for the natural end of human life would convince the world that the God who was born of you came into being also as perfect man, the Son of a true Mother, who was subject to the laws and constraints of nature, by divine decree and the requirement of an earthly lifetime. As one who possessed a human body you could not escape death, the common fate of humanity.

Thus even your Son, though God of all things, even he, through sharing, so to speak, the mortality of all our race, *tasted* a similar bodily *death*. It was clearly in the same way as he made his own life-giving tomb that he made your sepulcher wonderful also, as the tomb of your falling asleep, a tomb which received life; therefore both tombs really received your bodies, but could in no way affect them with corruption. For nor could you, as the vessel which contained God, waste away to dust in the destruction of death.

For since he who humbled himself in you was God from the beginning and eternal life, so the Mother of Life was to share the dwelling of Life, to accept her death like a sleep and consent to her translation like a waking, as the Mother of Life. For just as a child seeks and longs for its own mother, and the mother loves to spend her time with her child, so it was right that you, with your maternal love for your Son and God, should return to him. And it was right too that God, preserving a Son's love for you, should make his companionship with you into a perpetual association.

In this way, then, you suffered the death of finite beings and the translation to the immortal way of life of eternal beings where God dwells; and because you are his companion, Mother of God, you do not abandon your life with him.

Or:

From the apostolic constitution *Munificentissimus Deus* by Pope Pius XII

(AAS 42 [1950], 760-762, 767-769)

Your body is holy and excelling in splendor

The august Mother of God was mysteriously united from all eternity with Jesus Christ in one and the same decree of predestination, immaculate in her conception, a virgin inviolate in her divine motherhood, the wholehearted companion of the divine Redeemer who won complete victory over sin and its consequences.

Thus, she gained at last the supreme crown of her privileges—to be preserved immune from the corruption of the tomb, and, like her Son, when death had been conquered, to be carried up body and soul to the exalted glory of heaven, there to sit in splendor at the right hand of her Son, the immortal King of the ages.

RESPONSORY

The Virgin Mary is exalted above the choirs of angels.
— The Virgin Mary is exalted above the choirs of angels.

Blessed is the Lord who has raised her up.
— Above the choirs of angels.

Glory to the Father . . .
— The Virgin Mary is exalted above the choirs of angels.

Or:

As Mary is taken up to heaven,
the angels of God rejoice.
— As Mary is taken up to heaven,
the angels of God rejoice.

They worship the Lord and sing his praises.
— The angels of God rejoice.

Glory to the Father . . .
— As Mary is . . .

CANTICLE OF MARY Luke 1:46-55

Ant. Today the Virgin Mary was taken up to heaven; rejoice, for she reigns with Christ for ever.

Or: All generations will call me blessed: the Almighty has done great things for me.

My soul rejoices in the Lord

My soul proclaims the greatness of the Lord,
my spirit rejoices in God my Savior
for he has looked with favor on his lowly servant.

From this day all generations will call me blessed:
the Almighty has done great things for me,
and holy is his Name.

He has mercy on those who fear him
in every generation.

He has shown the strength of his arm,
he has scattered the proud in their conceit.

He has cast down the mighty from their thrones,
and has lifted up the lowly.

He has filled the hungry with good things,
and the rich he has sent away empty.

He has come to the help of his servant Israel
for he has remembered his promise of mercy,
the promise he made to our fathers,
to Abraham and his children for ever.

Glory to the Father, and to the Son, and to the Holy Spirit:
as it was in the beginning, is now, and will be for ever. Amen.

INTERCESSIONS

Let us praise God our almighty Father, who wished that Mary, his Son's mother, be celebrated by each generation. Now in need we ask:
Mary, full of grace, intercede for us.

O God, worker of miracles, you made the immaculate Virgin Mary share, body and soul, in your Son's glory in heaven,
— direct the hearts of your children to that same glory.

You made Mary our mother. Through her intercession grant strength to the weak, comfort to the sorrowing, pardon to sinners,
— salvation and peace to all.

You made Mary full of grace,
— grant all men the joyful abundance of your grace.

Make your Church of one mind and one heart in love,
— and help all those who believe to be one in prayer with Mary, the mother of Jesus.

You crowned Mary queen of heaven,
— may all the dead rejoice in your kingdom with the saints for ever.

Our Father . . .

CONCLUDING PRAYER

All-powerful and ever-living God,
you raised the sinless Virgin Mary,
mother of your Son,

body and soul to the glory of heaven.
May we see heaven as our final goal
and come to share her glory.

We ask this through our Lord Jesus Christ, your Son,
who lives and reigns with you and the Holy Spirit,
one God, for ever and ever.

May the Lord bless us,
protect us from all evil
and bring us to everlasting life.
—Amen.

OFFICE OF READINGS

Lord, open my lips.
— And my mouth will proclaim your praise.

Invitatory

Ant. Come, let us worship Christ, the Son of Mary.

Or: Come, let us sing to the Lord as we celebrate this feast of the Blessed Virgin Mary.

Psalm 95

A call to praise God

Encourage each other daily while it is still today (Hebrews 3:13)

(The antiphon is recited and then repeated)

Come, let us sing to the Lord
and shout with joy to the Rock who saves us.
Let us approach him with praise and thanksgiving
and sing joyful songs to the Lord.

(Antiphon repeated)

The Lord is God, the mighty God,
the great king over all the gods.
He holds in his hands the depths of the earth
and the highest mountains as well.
He made the sea; it belongs to him,
the dry land, too, for it was formed by his hands.

(Antiphon repeated)

Come, then, let us bow down and worship,
bending the knee before the Lord, our maker.
For he is our God and we are his people,
the flock he shepherds.

(Antiphon repeated)

Today, listen to the voice of the Lord:
Do not grow stubborn, as your fathers did
in the wilderness,
when at Meriba and Massah
they challenged me and provoked me,
Although they had seen all of my works.
(Antiphon repeated)

Forty years I endured that generation.
I said, "They are a people whose hearts go astray
and they do not know my ways."
So I swore in my anger,
"They shall not enter into my rest."
(Antiphon repeated)

Glory to the Father, and to the Son, and to the Holy Spirit:
as it was in the beginning, is now, and will be for ever. Amen.
(Antiphon repeated)

Office of Readings

God, come to my assistance.
— Lord, make haste to help me.
Glory to the Father, and to the Son, and to the Holy Spirit:
as it was in the beginning, is now, and will be for ever. Amen.

If the office begins with the invitatory, all the above is omitted.

HYMN

The God whom earth and sea and sky
Adore and laud and magnify,
Whose might they own, whose praise they tell,
In Mary's body deigned to dwell.

O Mother blest! the chosen shrine
Wherein the Architect divine,
Whose hand contains the earth and sky,
Vouchsafed in hidden guise to lie:

Blest in the message Gabriel brought;
Blest in the work the Spirit wrought;
Most blest, to bring to human birth
The long desired of all the earth.

O Lord, the Virgin born, to thee
Eternal praise and glory be,
Whom with the Father we adore
And Holy Ghost for ever more.

Melody: Eisenach L.M.
Music: Johan H. Schein, 1586-1630
Text: Venantius Fortunatus, 530-609
Translator: J.M. Neale, 1818-1866

Or:

Ye who own the faith of Jesus,
Sing the wonders that were done,
When the love of God the Father
O'er our sin the victory won,
When he made the Virgin Mary
Mother of his only Son.
Hail, Mary, full of grace.

Blessed were the chosen people
Out of whom the Lord did come,
Blessed was the land of promise
Fashioned for his earthly home;
But more blessed far the mother,
She who bore him in her womb.
Hail, Mary, full of grace.

Wherefore let all faithful people
Tell the honor of her name,
Let the Church in her foreshadowed
Part in her thanksgiving claim;
What Christ's mother sang in gladness—

Let Christ's people sing the same.
Hail, Mary, full of grace.

Praise, O Mary, praise the Father,
Praise thy Savior and thy Son,
Praise the everlasting Spirit,
Who hath made thee ark and throne.
O'er all creatures high exalted,
Lowly praise the three in one.
Hail, Mary, full of grace.

Melody: Den das Vaters Sinn geboren 87.87.876
Music: J.A. Freylinghausen, 1670-1739
Text: V.S.S. Coles, 1845-1929

PSALMODY

Ant. 1 Mary received a blessing from the Lord and loving kindness from God her savior.

Psalm 24
The Lord's entry into his temple

Christ opened heaven for us in the manhood he assumed (Saint Irenaeus).

The Lord's is the earth and its fullness,
the world and all its peoples.
It is he who set it on the seas;
on the waters he made it firm.

Who shall climb the mountain of the Lord?
Who shall stand in his holy place?
The man with clean hands and pure heart,
who desires not worthless things,
who has not sworn so as to deceive his neighbor.

He shall receive blessings from the Lord
and reward from the God who saves him.
Such are the men who seek him,
seek the face of the God of Jacob.

O gates, lift high your heads;
grow higher, ancient doors.
Let him enter, the king of glory!

Who is the king of glory?
The Lord, the mighty, the valiant,
the Lord, the valiant in war.

O gates, lift high your heads;
grow higher, ancient doors.
Let him enter, the king of glory!

Who is he, the king of glory?
He, the lord of armies,
he is the king of glory.

Ant. 2 The Most High has made his dwelling place a holy temple.

Psalm 46

God our refuge and strength

He shall be called Emmanuel, which means: God-with-us (Matthew 1:23).

God is for us a refuge and strength,
a helper close at hand, in time of distress:
so we shall not fear though the earth should rock,
though the mountains fall into the depths of the sea,
even though its waters rage and foam,
even though the mountains be shaken by its waves.

The Lord of hosts is with us:
the God of Jacob is our stronghold.

The waters of a river give joy to God's city,
the holy place where the Most High dwells.
God is within, it cannot be shaken;
God will help it at the dawning of the day.
Nations are in tumult, kingdoms are shaken:
he lifts his voice, the earth shrinks away.

The Lord of hosts is with us:
the God of Jacob is our stronghold.

Come, consider the works of the Lord,
the redoubtable deeds he has done on the earth.
He puts an end to wars over all the earth;
the bow he breaks, the spear he snaps.
He burns the shields with fire.
"Be still and know that I am God,
supreme among the nations, supreme on the earth!"

The Lord of hosts is with us:
the God of Jacob is our stronghold.

Ant. 3 Glorious things are said of you, O Virgin Mary.

Psalm 87

Jerusalem is mother of us all

The heavenly Jerusalem is a free woman; she is our mother (Galatians 4:26).

On the holy mountain is his city
cherished by the Lord.
The Lord prefers the gates of Zion
to all Jacob's dwellings.
Of you are told glorious things,
O city of God!

"Babylon and Egypt I will count
among those who know me;
Philistia, Tyre, Ethiopia,
these will be her children
and Zion shall be called 'Mother'
for all shall be her children."

It is he, the Lord Most High,
who gives each his place.
In his register of peoples he writes:
"These are her children,"
and while they dance they will sing:
"In you all find their home."

Blessed are those who hear the word of God.
— And cherish it in their hearts.

First Reading

From the letter of the apostle Paul
to the Galatians 3:22—4:7

Through faith we are the children and heirs of God

Scripture confined all things under the power of sin, that through faith in Jesus Christ the promise might be given to those who believe.

Before faith came, we were held in custody under law, confined for the faith that was to be revealed. Consequently, the law was our disciplinarian for Christ, that we might be justified by faith. But now that faith has come, we are no longer under a disciplinarian. For through faith you are all children of God in Christ Jesus. For all of you who were baptized into Christ have clothed yourselves with Christ. There is neither Jew nor Greek, there is neither slave nor free person, there is not male and female; for you are all one in Christ Jesus. And if you belong to Christ, then you are Abraham's descendant, heirs according to the promise.

I mean that as long as the heir is not of age, he is no different from a slave, although he is the owner of everything, but he is under the supervision of guardians and administrators until the date set by his father. In the same way we also, when we were not of age, were enslaved to the elemental powers of the world. But when the fullness of time had come, God sent his Son, born of a woman, born under the law, to ransom those under the law, so that we might receive adoption. As proof that you are children, God sent the spirit of his Son into our hearts, crying out, "Abba, Father!" So you are no longer a slave but a child, and if a child then also an heir, through God.

RESPONSORY See Gal 4:4-5; Eph 2:4; Rom 8:3

When the fullness of time had come,
God sent to earth his own Son,
born of a woman, subject to the law;
— to deliver those under the law.

Because of his great love for us,
God sent his own Son
in the likeness of our sinful flesh.
— To deliver those . . . .

SECOND READING

From a sermon by Saint Aelred, abbot

(Sermo 20, in Nativitate beatae Mariae: PL 195, 322-324)

Mary our mother

Let us come to his bride, his mother, his perfect handmaid, for the blessed Mary is all of this.

But what are we to do for her? What kind of gifts shall we offer her? Would that we could at least return what we are in duty bound to do, for we owe her honor and service, we owe her love and praise. We owe her honor, for she is the mother of our Lord. He who fails to honor the mother clearly dishonors the son. Also, Scripture says: *Honor your father and your mother.*

What then, my brothers, shall we say? Is she not our mother? Yes, my brothers, she is indeed our mother, for through her we have been born, not for the world but for God.

Once we all lay in death, as you know and believe, in sin, in darkness, in misery. In death, because we had lost the Lord; in sin, because of our corruption; in darkness, for we were without the light of wisdom, and thus had perished utterly.

But then we were born, far better than through Eve, through Mary the blessed, because Christ was born of her. We have recovered new life in place of sin, immortality instead of mortality, light in place of darkness.

She is our mother—the mother of our life, the mother of our incarnation, the mother of our light. As the Apostle says of our Lord, *he became for us by God's power our wisdom and justice, and holiness and redemption.*

She then, as mother of Christ, is the mother of our wisdom and justice, of our holiness and redemption. She is more our mother than the mother of our flesh. Our birth from her is better, for from her is born our holiness, our wisdom, our justice, our sanctification, our redemption.

Praise the Lord in his holy ones, say the Scriptures. If our Lord is to be praised in those holy ones through whom he brings to being deeds of power and miracles, how much more is he to be praised in her in whom he fashioned himself, who is wonderful beyond all wonders.

RESPONSORY

Happy are you, holy Virgin Mary, and most worthy of all praise;
— from your womb Christ the Sun of Justice has risen.
Through him we have salvation and deliverance.

Let us celebrate with joy this feast in honor of the Blessed Virgin Mary.
— From your womb . . .

Alternative:

From the dogmatic constitution on the Church of the Second Vatican Council

(Lumen gentium, nn. 61-62)

Mary's motherhood in the order of grace

This motherhood of Mary in the order of grace—from the consent which she gave in faith at the annunciation, and which she continued to give unhesitatingly at the foot of the cross—lasts without interruption until all the elect enter into eternal fulfillment. When she was taken up into heaven, she did not lay aside this saving role but she continues by her intercession for all to gain for us the gifts of eternal salvation.

In her maternal love she cares for the brothers and sisters of her Son as they journey on earth in the midst of dangers and hardships, until they are brought safely home to the happiness of heaven.

The Blessed Virgin is thus invoked in the Church under the titles of Advocate, Auxiliatrix, Adjutrix and Mediatrix. These titles must not, however, be understood as in any way detracting from, or adding to, the dignity and effectiveness of Christ, the one Mediator.

No creature can ever be classed as an equal with the incarnate Word, the Redeemer. But just as the priesthood of Christ is shared in various ways by his ministers and his faithful people, and as the goodness of God, one though it is, is in different ways, really shared with creatures, so also the unique mediation of Christ does not exclude but brings about a variety of shared cooperation, deriving from the one unique source.

The Church does not hesitate to acknowledge this kind of subordinate role in the person of Mary. The Church has continuous experience of its effects, and commends it to the hearts of the faithful, so that as they lean on her motherly protection they may be brought into closer union with the Mediator, our Savior.

Responsory

O pure and holy Virgin, how can I find words to praise your beauty?
— The highest heavens cannot contain God whom you carried in your womb.

Blessed are you among women, and blessed is the fruit of your womb.
— The highest heavens . . .

Hymn, Te Deum

For Sundays, solemnities, and feasts, the hymn Te Deum follows the second reading and its responsory.

You are God: we praise you;
You are the Lord: we acclaim you;
You are the eternal Father:
All creation worships you.

To you all angels, all the powers of heaven,
Cherubim and Seraphim, sing in endless praise:
Holy, holy, holy, Lord, God of power and might,
heaven and earth are full of your glory.

The glorious company of apostles praise you.
The noble fellowship of prophets praise you.
The white-robed army of martyrs praise you.

Throughout the world the holy Church acclaims you:
Father, of majesty unbounded,
your true and only Son, worthy of all worship,
and the Holy Spirit, advocate and guide.

You, Christ, are the king of glory,
the eternal Son of the Father.

When you became man to set us free
you did not spurn the Virgin's womb.

You overcame the sting of death,
and opened the kingdom of heaven to all believers.

You are seated at God's right hand in glory.
We believe that you will come, and be our judge.

Come, then, Lord, and help your people,
bought with the price of your own blood, —

and bring us with your saints
to glory everlasting.

℣. Save your people, Lord, and bless your inheritance.
℟. Govern and uphold them now and always.
℣. Day by day we bless you.
℟. We praise your name for ever.
℣. Keep us today, Lord, from all sin.
℟. Have mercy on us, Lord, have mercy.
℣. Lord, show us your love and mercy;
℟. for we put our trust in you.
℣. In you, Lord, is our hope:
℟. and we shall never hope in vain.

Concluding Prayer

Lord our God,
you have made the Virgin Mary
the model for all who welcome your word
and who put it into practice.
Open our hearts to receive it with joy
and by the power of your Spirit
grant that we also may become a dwelling place
in which your Word of salvation is fulfilled.

We ask this through our Lord Jesus Christ, your Son,
who lives and reigns with you and the Holy Spirit,
one God, for ever and ever.

Let us praise the Lord.
— And give him thanks.

DAYTIME PRAYER

God, come to my assistance.
— Lord, make haste to help me.

Glory to the Father, and to the Son, and to the Holy Spirit:
as it was in the beginning, is now, and will be for ever. Amen.

HYMN

Midmorning

Breathe on me, breath of God,
Fill me with life anew,
That I may love the things you love,
And do what you would do.

Breathe on me, breath of God,
Until my heart is pure,
Until with you I have one will,
To live and to endure.

Breathe on me, breath of God,
My soul with grace refine,
Until this earthly part of me
Glows with your fire divine.

Breathe on me, breath of God,
So I shall never die,
But live with you the perfect life
In your eternity.

Melody: Yattendon 46

Music: H. E. Wooldridge, 1845-1917
Text: Edwin Hatch, 1835-1889, adapted by Anthony G. Petti

Or:

From all that dwell below the skies
Let the Creator's praise arise:
Let the Redeemer's name be sung
Through every land, by every tongue,
Hallelujah!

Eternal are thy mercies, Lord;
Eternal truth attends thy word:
Thy praise shall sound from shore to shore,
Till suns shall rise and set no more:
Hallelujah!

Melody: Erschienen ist der herrliche Tag or Eisenach (without hallelujah) L.M.

Music: Nikolaus Hermann, 1560 or Johan H. Schein, 1583-1630
Text: Isaac Watts, 1719

Midday

Help us, O Lord, to learn
The truths thy Word imparts:
To study that thy laws may be
Inscribed upon our hearts.

Help us, O Lord, to live
The faith which we proclaim,
That all our thoughts and words and deeds
May glorify your name.

Help us, O Lord, to teach
The beauty of your ways,
That yearning souls may find the Christ,
And sing aloud his praise.

Melody: Franconia S.M.

Music: J. B. König, 1691-1758, adapted by W. H. Havergal, 1793-1870
Text: W. W. Reid, 1923-

Or:

Lord of all hopefulness, Lord of all joy,
Whose trust, ever childlike, no cares could destroy,
Be there at our waking, and give us, we pray,
Your bliss in our hearts, Lord, at the break of the day.

Lord of all eagerness, Lord of all faith,
Whose strong hands were skilled at the plane and the lathe,

Be there at our labors, and give us, we pray,
Your strength in our hearts, Lord, at the noon of the day.

Lord of all kindliness, Lord of all grace,
Your hand swift to welcome, your arms to embrace,
Be there at our homing, and give us, we pray,
Your love in our hearts, Lord, at the eve of the day.

Lord of all gentleness, Lord of all calm,
Whose voice is contentment, whose presence is balm,
Be there at our sleeping, and give us, we pray,
Your peace in our hearts, Lord, at the end of the day.

Melody: Slane 10.11.11.12
Music: Irish Traditional Melody
Text: Jan Struther, 1901-1953

Midafternoon

Firmly I believe and truly
God is three and God is one;
And I next acknowledge duly
Manhood taken by the Son.

And I trust and hope most fully
In that manhood crucified;
And I love supremely, solely
Christ who for my sins has died.

And I hold in veneration,
For the love of him alone,
Holy Church as his creation,
And her teachings as his own.

Praise and thanks be ever given
With and through the angel host,
To the God of earth and heaven,
Father, Son and Holy Ghost.

Melody: Halton Holgate
87.87
Music: William Boyce, 1710-1779
Text: John Henry Newman, 1801-1890
adapted by Anthony G. Petti

Or:

Lord God and Maker of all things,
Creation is upheld by you.
While all must change and know decay,
You are unchanging, always new.

You are man's solace and his shield,
His rock secure on which to build;
You are the spirit's tranquil home;
In you alone is hope fulfilled.

To God the Father and the Son
And Holy Spirit render praise,
Blest Trinity, from age to age
The strength of all our living days.

Melody: Auctoritate Saeculi L.M. Music: *Poitiers Antiphoner,* 1746
Text: Stanbrook Abbey

Midmorning

Ant. All of them, united in heart, continued in prayer, with Mary the mother of Jesus.

Midday

Ant. The mother of Jesus said: Do whatever he asks of you.

Midafternoon

Ant. The Lord said to his mother: Woman, this is your son, and to the disciple: This is your mother.

PSALMODY

Ant. 1 Lead me, Lord, in the path of your commandments.

Psalm 119:33-40

V (He)

Teach me the demands of your precepts
and I will keep them to the end.—

Train me to observe your law,
to keep it with my heart.

Guide me in the path of your commands;
for there is my delight.
Bend my heart to your will
and not to love of gain.

Keep my eyes from what is false:
by your word, give me life.
Keep the promise you have made
to the servant who fears you.

Keep me from the scorn I dread,
for your decrees are good.
See, I long for your precepts:
then in your justice, give me life.

Ant. 2 Those who seek the Lord will be filled with every blessing.

Psalm 34

God the savior of the just

You have tasted the sweetness of the Lord (1 Peter 2:3).

I

I will bless the Lord at all times,
his praise always on my lips;
in the Lord my soul shall make its boast.
The humble shall hear and be glad.

Glorify the Lord with me.
Together let us praise his name.
I sought the Lord and he answered me;
from all my terrors he set me free.

Look towards him and be radiant;
let your faces not be abashed. —

This poor man called; the Lord heard him
and rescued him from all his distress.

The angel of the Lord is encamped
around those who revere him, to rescue them.
Taste and see that the Lord is good.
He is happy who seeks refuge in him.

Revere the Lord, you his saints.
They lack nothing, those who revere him.
Strong lions suffer want and go hungry
but those who seek the Lord lack no blessing.

Ant. 3 Seek and strive after peace.

II

Come, children, and hear me
that I may teach you the fear of the Lord.
Who is he who longs for life
and many days, to enjoy his prosperity?

Then keep your tongue from evil
and your lips from seeking deceit.
Turn aside from evil and do good;
seek and strive after peace.

The Lord turns his face against the wicked
to destroy their remembrance from the earth.
The Lord turns his eyes to the just
and his ears to their appeal.

They call and the Lord hears
and rescues them in all their distress.
The Lord is close to the broken-hearted;
those whose spirit is crushed he will save.

Many are the trials of the just man
but from them all the Lord will rescue him.
He will keep guard over all his bones,
not one of his bones shall be broken.

Evil brings death to the wicked;
those who hate the good are doomed.
The Lord ransoms the souls of his servants.
Those who hide in him shall not be condemned.

Midmorning

FIRST READING Zephaniah 3:14, 15

Shout for joy, O daughter Zion!
sing joyfully, O Israel!
Be glad and exult with all your heart,
O daughter Jerusalem!
The King of Israel, the Lord,
is in your midst.

SECOND READING

From a homily by Saint Ambrose, bishop

Let Mary's soul be in each of you

Elizabeth was filled with the Holy Spirit after conceiving a son; Mary was filled before. "You are blessed," said Elizabeth, "because you have believed."

You too are blessed because you have heard and believed. The soul of every believer conceives and brings forth the Word of God and recognizes his works. Let Mary's soul be in each of you to glorify the Lord. Let her spirit be in each of you to rejoice in the Lord. Christ has only one Mother in the flesh, but we all bring forth Christ by faith. Every soul free from contamination of sin and inviolate in its purity can receive the Word of God.

Blessed are those who hear the word of God.
— And cherish it in their hearts.

Midday

FIRST READING Zechariah 9:9

Rejoice heartily, O daughter Zion,
shout for joy, O daughter Jerusalem.
See, your king shall come to you;
a just savior is he.

SECOND READING

From a homily by Saint Peter Chrysologus, bishop

Let no one judge in a human way
what is done in a divine mystery

A virgin conceived and a virgin brought forth her child. Do not be disturbed at this conception or confused when you hear of this birth. Let no one judge in a human way what is done in a divine mystery. Let no one try to penetrate this heavenly mystery by earthly reasoning. Let no one treat this novel secret from knowledge of everyday occurrences. Let no one manipulate the work of love into an insult, or run the risk of losing faith.

Blessed is the womb of the Virgin Mary.
— Who bore the Son of the Eternal Father.

Midafternoon

FIRST READING Judith 13:31

Blessed are you in every tent of Judah; and in every foreign nation, all who hear of you will be struck with terror.

SECOND READING

From a homily by an unknown Greek author

Mary is celebrated in the sacred words of Scripture

Mary stood at your right hand, robed in a gown of gold, with adornment intricately wrought. Just as, being a woman, she was named queen and lady and Mother of God, so also now, standing as queen at the right hand of her most regal Son, she is celebrated in the sacred words of Scripture as clothed in the golden gown of incorruptibility. And so as we gaze upon him who is our king and lord and God, and upon her who is queen and lady and the Mother of God, contemplating them with the clear-sighted eye of our minds, let us repeat again and again unceasingly: The queen stands at your right hand, robed in a gown of gold with adornment intricately wrought.

Blessed are you among women.
— And blessed is the fruit of your womb.

Concluding Prayer

Lord,
make the peace we pray for a reality:
may we live our days in quiet joy
and, with the help of the Virgin Mary's prayers,
safely reach your kingdom.

Grant this through Christ our Lord.

Or:

Gracious God and Father,
in Mary, the first-born of redemption,
you have given us a Mother most tender.
Open our hearts to the joy of the Spirit,
and grant that by imitating the Virgin
we too may learn to magnify you
through the great work accomplished in Christ, your Son.

He lives and reigns with you and the Holy Spirit,
one God, for ever and ever.

Or:

Holy and merciful God,
you are pleased by the humble
and accomplish in them by means of the Spirit
the great wonders of salvation.
Look upon the innocence of the Virgin Mary,
and give us simple and generous hearts
that respond without hesitation to every sign of your will.

Grant this through our Lord Jesus Christ, your Son,
who lives and reigns with you and the Holy Spirit,
one God, for ever and ever.

In the communal celebration of the office, the acclamation is added:

Let us praise the Lord.
— And give him thanks.

NIGHT PRAYER

INTRODUCTION

God, come to my assistance.

— Lord, make haste to help me.

Glory to the Father, and to the Son, and to the Holy Spirit:

as it was in the beginning, is now, and will be for ever. Amen.

A brief examination of conscience may be made. At its conclusion one of the penitential prayers may be said.

1.

I confess to almighty God,
and to you, my brothers and sisters,
that I have sinned through my own fault
in my thoughts and in my words,
in what I have done,
and in what I have failed to do;
and I ask blessed Mary, ever virgin,
all the angels and saints,
and you, my brothers and sisters,
to pray for me to the Lord our God.

2.

My God,
I am sorry for my sins with all my heart.
In choosing to do wrong
and failing to do good,
I have sinned against you
whom I should love above all things.
I firmly intend, with your help,
to do penance,
to sin no more,
and to avoid whatever leads me to sin.
Our Savior Jesus Christ

suffered and died for us.
In his name, my God, have mercy.

3.

Remember, Lord, your compassion and mercy
which you showed long ago.
Do not recall the sins and failings of my youth.
In your mercy remember me, Lord, because of your goodness.

Psalm 25:6-7

Hymn

O Christ, you are the light and day
Which drives away the night,
The ever shining Sun of God
And pledge of future light.

As now the ev'ning shadows fall
Please grant us, Lord, we pray,
A quiet night to rest in you
Until the break of day.

Remember us, poor mortal men,
We humbly ask, O Lord,
And may your presence in our souls
Be now our great reward.

Melody: Saint Anne C.M.
Music: William Croft, 1708
Text: Christe qui Lux es et Dies
Translator: Rev. M. Quinn, O.P., et al.

Psalmody

Ant. Night holds no terrors for me sleeping under God's wings.

Psalm 91

Safe in God's sheltering care

I have given you the power to tread upon serpents and scorpions (Luke 10:19).

He who dwells in the shelter of the Most High
and abides in the shade of the Almighty
says to the Lord: "My refuge,
my stronghold, my God in whom I trust!"

It is he who will free you from the snare
of the fowler who seeks to destroy you;
he will conceal you with his pinions
and under his wings you will find refuge.

You will not fear the terror of the night
nor the arrow that flies by day,
nor the plague that prowls in the darkness
nor the scourge that lays waste at noon.

A thousand may fall at your side,
ten thousand fall at your right,
you, it will never approach;
his faithfulness is buckler and shield.

Your eyes have only to look
to see how the wicked are repaid,
you who have said: "Lord, my refuge!"
and have made the Most High your dwelling.

Upon you no evil shall fall,
no plague approach where you dwell.
For you has he commanded his angels,
to keep you in all your ways.

They shall bear you upon their hands
lest you strike your foot against a stone.
On the lion and the viper you will tread
and trample the young lion and the dragon.

Since he clings to me in love, I will free him;
protect him for he knows my name.
When he calls I shall answer: "I am with you."
I will save him in distress and give him glory.

With length of life I will content him;
I shall let him see my saving power.

First Reading — Revelation 22:4-5

They will look upon his face, and his name will be on their foreheads. Night will be no more, nor will they need light from lamp or sun, for the Lord God shall give them light, and they shall reign forever and ever.

Second Reading

From a homily by Saint Bede the Venerable, priest

(Lib. 1, 4: CCL 122, 25-26. 30)

Remembering the example of God's Mother

By meditating upon the incarnation, our devotion is kindled, and by remembering the example of God's Mother, we are encouraged to lead a life of virtue. Such virtues are best achieved in the evening. We are weary after the day's work and worn out by our distractions. The time for rest is near, and our minds are ready for contemplation.

Responsory

Into your hands, Lord, I commend my spirit.
— Into your hands, Lord, I commend my spirit.

You have redeemed us, Lord God of truth.
— I commend my spirit.

Glory to the Father . . .
— Into your hands . . .

Ant. Protect us, Lord, as we stay awake; watch over us as we sleep, that awake, we may keep watch with Christ, and asleep, rest in his peace.

Gospel Canticle — Luke 2:29-32

Christ is the light of the nations and the glory of Israel

Lord, now you let your servant go in peace;
your word has been fulfilled:

my own eyes have seen the salvation
which you have prepared in the sight of every people:

a light to reveal you to the nations
and the glory of your people Israel.

Glory to the Father . . .

Concluding Prayer

Father of holiness,
for the journey of your pilgrim Church on earth,
you have provided the Virgin Mary as a sign and beacon.
Through her intercession
sustain our faith and enliven our hope,
that no obstacle may divert us
from the road which brings us salvation.

Grant this through Christ our Lord.

Or:

God and Father of Christ our Savior,
in Mary, the holy Virgin and attentive Mother,
you have given us the image of your Church.
Send your Spirit to help our weakness,
that we may persevere in faith, grow in love,
and walk together to the heaven of blessed hope.

We ask this through Christ our Lord.

Conclusion

May the all-powerful Lord grant us a restful night
and a peaceful death.
— Amen.

ANTIPHONS OF THE BLESSED VIRGIN MARY

Advent

Alma Redemptoris Mater

Loving mother of the Redeemer,
gate of heaven, star of the sea,
assist your people who have fallen yet strive to rise again.
To the wonderment of nature you bore your Creator,
yet remained a virgin after as before.
You who received Gabriel's joyful greeting,
have pity on us poor sinners.

> Alma Redemptoris Mater, quae pervia caeli
> porta manes, et stella maris, sucurre cadenti,
> surgere qui curat, populo: tu quae genuisti,
> natura mirante, tuum sanctum Genitorem,
> Virgo prius ac posterius, Gabrielis ab ore
> sumens illud Ave, peccatorum miserere.

Lent

Ave Regina Caelorum

Hail, Queen of heaven;
Hail, Mistress of the Angels;
Hail, root of Jesse;
Hail, the gate through which the Light rose over the earth.
Rejoice, Virgin most renowned and of unsurpassed beauty.

> Ave, Regina caelorum,
> ave, Domina angelorum,
> salve, radix, salve, porta,
> ex qua mundo lux est orta.
>
> Gaude, Virgo gloriosa,
> super omnes speciosa;

vale, O valde decora,
et pro nobis Christum exora.

Easter

Regina Caeli

Queen of heaven, rejoice, alleluia.
The Son whom you merited to bear, alleluia,
has risen as he said, alleluia.
Pray to God for us, alleluia.

Rejoice and be glad, O Virgin Mary, alleluia.
For the Lord has truly risen, alleluia.

Regina caeli, laetare, alleluia:
quia quem meruisti portare, alleluia.
Resurrexit, sicut dixit, alleluia.
Ora pro nobis Deum, alleluia.

Gaude et laetare, Virgo Maria, alleluia.
Quia surrexit Dominus vere, alleluia.

Salve, Regina

Hail, holy Queen, Mother of mercy,
hail, our life, our sweetness, and our hope.
To you we cry, the children of Eve;
to you we send up our sighs,
mourning and weeping in this land of exile.
Turn, then, most gracious advocate,
your eyes of mercy toward us;
lead us home at last
and show us the blessed fruit of your womb, Jesus:
O clement, O loving, O sweet Virgin Mary.

Salve, Regina, mater misericordiae;
vita, dulcedo et spes nostra, salve.
Ad te clamamus, exsules filii Evae.
Ad te suspiramus, gementes et flentes
in hac lacrimarum valle.

Eia ergo, advocata nostra,
illos tuos misericordes oculos ad nos converte.
Et Iesum, benedictum fructum ventris tui,
nobis post hoc exsilium ostende.
O clemens, o pia, o dulcis Virgo Maria.

THANKSGIVING FOR MARY'S FIAT

For Mary's role in salvation history one may wish to give thanks and praise to God with the following meditation: canticles, a reading from the gospel, the hymn of praise, and a prayer. This thanksgiving may be said at any time. It may be used as a beginning point for reflection on the mystery of Christ's coming for all nations.

Ant. Be glad, Virgin Mary, for you have deserved to bear the Christ, the creator of heaven and earth; you have brought forth the Savior of the world.

Canticle I Isaiah 61:10--62:3

The prophet rejoices over the new Jerusalem

I saw the new Jerusalem, the holy city, prepared as a bride adorned for her bridegroom (Revelation 21:2).

I rejoice heartily in the Lord,
in my God is the joy of my soul;
for he has clothed me with a robe of salvation,
and wrapped me in a mantle of justice,
like a bridegroom adorned with a diadem,
like a bride bedecked with her jewels.

As the earth brings forth its plants,
and a garden makes its growth spring up,
so will the Lord God make justice and praise
spring up before all the nations.

For Zion's sake I will not be silent,
for Jerusalem's sake I will not be quiet,
until her vindication shines forth like the dawn
and her victory like a burning torch.

Nations shall behold your vindication,
and all kings your glory;
you shall be called by a new name
pronounced by the mouth of the Lord.

You shall be a glorious crown in the hand of the Lord,
a royal diadem held by your God.

Canticle II — Isaiah 62:4-7

The glory of the new Jerusalem

Here God lives among men. He will make his home among them (Revelation 21:3).

No more shall men call you "Forsaken,"
or your land "Desolate,"
but you shall be called "My Delight,"
and your land "Espoused."
For the Lord delights in you,
and makes your land his spouse.

As a young man marries a virgin,
your Builder shall marry you;
and as a bridegroom rejoices in his bride
so shall your God rejoice in you.

Upon your walls, O Jerusalem,
I have stationed watchmen;
Never, by day or by night,
shall they be silent.

O you who are to remind the Lord,
take no rest
and give no rest to him,
until he re-establishes Jerusalem
and makes it
the pride of the earth.

Canticle III — Sirach 39:13-16a

How praiseworthy are the works of the Lord!

Thanks be to God who through us is spreading the knowledge of himself like a pleasant fragrance (2 Corinthians 2:14).

Listen, my faithful children: open up your petals,
like roses planted near running waters;
send up the sweet odor of incense,
break forth in blossoms like the lily.

Send up the sweet odor of your hymn of praise;
bless the Lord for all he has done!

Proclaim the greatness of his name,
loudly sing his praises,
with music on the harp and all stringed instruments;
sing out with joy as you proclaim:
The works of God are all of them good.

Ant. Be glad, Virgin Mary, for you have deserved to bear the Christ, the creator of heaven and earth; you have brought forth the Savior of the world.

Gospel from the common of the Blessed Virgin Mary from the Lectionary for Mass.

Luke 1:26-38

A reading from the holy gospel
according to Luke

You will conceive and bear a son.

In the sixth month, the angel Gabriel was sent from God to a town of Galilee called Nazareth, to a virgin betrothed to a man named Joseph, of the house of David, and the virgin's name was Mary. And coming to her, he said, "Hail, favored one! The Lord is with you." But she was greatly troubled at what was said and pondered what sort of greeting this might be. Then the angel said to her, "Do not be afraid, Mary, for you have found favor with God. Behold, you will conceive in your womb and bear a son, and you shall name him Jesus. He will be great and will be called Son of the Most High, and the Lord God will give him the throne of David his father, and he will rule over the house of Jacob forever, and of his kingdom there will be no end." But Mary said to the angel, "How can this be, since I have no relations with a man?" And the angel said to her in reply, "The holy Spirit will come upon you, and the power of the Most High will overshadow you. Therefore the child to be born will be called holy, the Son of God. And behold, Elizabeth, your relative, has also conceived a son in her old age, and this is the sixth month for her who was called barren; for nothing will be impossible for God." Mary said, "Behold, I am the handmaid of the Lord. May it be done to me according to your word." Then the angel departed from her.

Luke 1:39-47

A reading from the holy gospel
according to Luke

Blessed are you who believed.

During those days Mary set out and traveled to the hill country in haste to a town of Judah, where she entered the house of Zechariah and greeted Elizabeth. When Elizabeth heard Mary's greeting, the infant leaped in her womb, and Elizabeth, filled with the holy Spirit, cried out in a loud voice and said, "Most blessed are you among women, and blessed is the fruit of your womb. And how does this happen to me, that the mother of my Lord should come to me? For at the moment the sound of your greeting reached my ears, the infant in my womb leaped for joy. Blessed are you who believed that what was spoken to you by the Lord would be fulfilled."

And Mary said:

"My soul proclaims the greatness of the Lord;
my spirit rejoices in God my savior."

Luke 2:15-19

A reading from the holy gospel
according to Luke

Mary kept all these things, reflecting on them in her heart.

The shepherds said to one another, "Let us go, then, to Bethlehem to see this thing that has taken place, which the Lord has made known to us." So they went in haste and found Mary and Joseph, and the infant lying in the manger. When they saw this, they made known the message that had been told them about this child. All who heard it were amazed by what had been told them by the shepherds. And Mary kept all these things, reflecting on them in her heart.

Luke 2:27-35

A reading from the holy gospel
according to Luke

And you yourself a sword will pierce.

Simeon came in the Spirit into the temple; and when the parents brought in the child Jesus to perform the custom of the law in regard to him, he took him into his arms and blessed God, saying:

"Now, Master, you may let your servant go
  in peace, according to your word,
for my eyes have seen your salvation,
  which you prepared in sight of all the peoples,
a light for revelation to the Gentiles,
  and glory for your people Israel."

The child's father and mother were amazed at what was said about him; and Simeon blessed them and said to Mary his mother, "Behold, this child is destined for the fall and rise of many in Israel, and to be a sign that will be contradicted (and you yourself a sword will pierce) so that the thoughts of many hearts may be revealed."

Luke 11:27-28

A reading from the holy gospel
according to Luke

Blessed is the womb that carried you!

While Jesus was speaking, a woman from the crowd called out and said to him, "Blessed is the womb that carried you and the breasts at which you nursed." He replied, "Rather, blessed are those who hear the word of God and observe it."

John 19:25-27

A reading from the holy gospel
according to John

Woman, behold, your son. Behold, your mother.

Standing by the cross of Jesus were his mother and his mother's sister, Mary the wife of Clopas, and Mary of Magdala. When Jesus saw his mother and the disciple there whom he loved, he said to his mother, "Woman, behold, your son." Then he said to the disciple, "Behold, your mother." And from that hour the disciple took her into his home.

READING

From a sermon by Saint Thomas of Villanova, bishop

(Sermon on the Birth of Mary, II, 7-9)

Let us place ourselves under Mary's protection

What joy, what happiness there is in heaven! The shoot from the root of Jesse, sown so long ago in the time of the patriarchs, has today sprung up and begun to grow, and will bear a Flower which is destined to heal the world, a Flower whose scent revives the dead, whose taste heals the sick, and whose beauty delights the angels—a white and red Flower *which angels long to see.*

As Bernard says: "Rejoice, father Adam, but even more you, mother Eve, exult, who as you were the parents of all were also the destroyers of all, and what is worse, destroyers before you were parents. So both of you must take comfort from your daughter, and such a daughter too. What was it, Adam, you said? *It was the woman who gave me fruit from the tree, and so I ate it.* Now today a woman is returned to you for a woman, a prudent woman for a foolish one, a humble for a proud, one who is to offer you the taste of life instead of the tree of death, and produce the sweetness of eternal fruit instead of the bitterness of that poisonous food. A virgin to be admired and most worthy of every honor! A woman to be uniquely revered, wonderful above all women, the savior of her parents and giver of life to her descendants."

Let us then throw ourselves at the feet of this holy Sibyl, and pour out our prayers with exultant spirit and sing praises while our hearts dance with joy: let us place ourselves under her protection, and cry aloud: *Therefore, you our Advocate,* Our Lady, our delight, *therefore turn your merciful eyes toward us, and after this our exile show us Jesus, the blessed fruit of your womb.* It is him we seek, him we gasp for, hastening toward him, desiring him with all the ardor of our hearts. It is you, Virgin, who must direct us, you must lead us to him, lead us to where he reigns, and show him to us, crowned with glory and honor, surrounded by angels, seated on the highest throne at the right hand of the Father, reigning with him, and governing the whole world together with him.

For a long time I have wondered and been at a loss to understand why the evangelists should have spoken at such length about John the Baptist and the other apostles, and yet told us so little about the Virgin Mary, who in life and distinction excels them all. Being at a loss, as I say, to understand this, all I can think is that it pleased the Holy Spirit that it should be so. It was by the providence of the Holy Spirit that the evangelists kept silent, because the glory of the Virgin, as we read in the psalms, was all within, and could more truly be thought of than described. The outline of her life: that *Jesus was born* of her, is enough to tell her whole story. What more do you seek for in the Virgin? It is enough for you that she is the Mother of God. What beauty, I ask you, what virtue, what perfection, what grace, what glory does not belong to the Mother of God?

The Holy Spirit has not described her in words, but has left her to you to picture in your own mind, so that you may understand that there was nothing she lacked of grace, perfection, or glory which could be imagined in the mind of a chaste human being, or rather that in fact she surpassed all understanding. So when she was wholly perfect, it would not have been right to describe her in part, for fear that you might think she could have lacked what had not been described. To say of the Virgin Mary only that she is the Mother of God surpasses all that can be said under God.

What a marvelous woman, to be the mother of her own Creator! What an amazing distinction for a woman, to have a Son in common with God. The Father loves his Son; the Mother rejoices in her Son. The Father tells his Son: *From the womb, before the morning star, I begot you;* the Mother says to her same Son: From the womb, I, a virgin, brought you into the world. She is amazed at her own glory, nor can she herself understand her elevation, for by the very fact of being made mother of the Creator she became with the best right mistress and queen of all creation. Truly, Mary, *he who is powerful did great things* for you; truly because he made you his own mother, *all the generations* of the ages *will call you blessed.*

Reading

From a homily of Blessed Simon of Cascia, priest

Present in spirit at the annunciation

Imagine how reverently the angel stood before this glorious village girl, knowing that she was to be the mother of the Son of God! See and contemplate how humbly and modestly she listened and gave answer to the angel who had come as ambassador and was awaiting her reply.

What would you have done if you had been at the door of this room or cell and had heard this holy, pleasing dialogue between this blessed girl and the angel? Would not your heart have been sweetly riven by great joy and boundless consolation? Harder than stone and steel is the heart that is not riven as it reads or hears or thinks about the words the virgin spoke to the angel and the angel to the virgin. Would you not have cried aloud, humbly but very fervently and from a full heart: "Sweet Madonna, kindest of women, I beg you, agree quickly to what the angel says, so that your Son may deliver us from the damnation in which our first mother has put us!"

What would you have said and done, Christian soul, when you heard the Virgin Mary say to the angel: "I am the servant and handmaiden of the Lord; be it done to me according to your word"? At that moment, the power of the Holy Spirit immediately formed and generated the body of Christ from the pure blood of the Virgin, infused the newly created soul into that body, and united the divinity inseparably with that soul and body. We must therefore firmly believe that Christ is true God and true man, the Son of Mary who was a virgin before, during, and after his birth. Those who do not believe this will be damned, unless they are converted to the true faith.

Reading

From a homily by Basil of Seleucia, bishop

(Oratio 39, 4. 5: PG 85, 438. 442. 446)

The Mother of God outshines all the martyrs

Born of the Virgin Mother of God, the Creator and Lord of all shared our human nature, for he had a real body and soul even though he had no part in our misdeeds. *He committed no sin,* says Scripture, *and no falsehood ever came from his mouth.* O holy womb in which God was received, in which the record of our sins was effaced, in which God became man while remaining God! He was carried in the womb, condescending to be born in the same way as we are. Yet when he was received into the arms of his mother he did not leave the bosom of his Father. God is not divided as he carries out his will, but saves the world without suffering any division in himself. When Gabriel came into the presence of the Virgin Mother of God he left heaven behind, but when the Word of God who fills all creation took flesh within her, he was not separated from the adoring hosts of heaven.

Is there any need to enumerate all the prophecies foretelling Christ's birth of the Mother of God? What tongue could worthily hymn her through whom we have received such magnificent blessings? With what flowers of praise could we weave a fitting crown for her from whom sprang the flower of Jesse, who has crowned our race with glory and honor. What gifts could we bring that would be worthy of her of whom the whole world is unworthy? If Paul could say of the other saints that the world was not worthy of them, what can we say of the Mother of God, who outshines all the martyrs even as the sun outshines the stars?

O Virgin, well may the angels rejoice in you! Because of you they who long ages ago had banished our race are now sent to our service, and to his joy Gabriel is entrusted with the news of a divine child's conception. *Rejoice, most favored one,* let your face glow with gladness. You are to give birth to the joy of all the world, who will put an end to the age-old curse, destroying the power of death and giving to all the hope of resurrection.

HYMN, Te Deum, 155.

CONCLUDING PRAYER

God and Father of the Lord Jesus Christ,
look upon the Virgin Mary,
whose earthly existence was governed
by a spirit of gracious acceptance.
Grant to us also
the gifts of constant prayer and of silence,
that our daily lives may be transfigured
by the presence of your Spirit.

We ask this through our Lord Jesus Christ, your Son,
who lives and reigns with you and the Holy Spirit,
one God, for ever and ever.

Let us praise the Lord.
And give him thanks.

PRAYERS TO THE BLESSED VIRGIN MARY

The Angelic Salutation

The "Hail Mary" ("Ave Maria") is based on Luke 1:28, 42 and is known as the "Angelic Salutation" from its first line.

Hail Mary, full of grace,
the Lord is with you!
Blessed are you among women,
and blessed is the fruit of your womb, Jesus.
Holy Mary, Mother of God,
pray for us sinners,
now and at the hour of our death.
Amen.

Ancient Prayer to the Virgin

This prayer, known in Latin as "Sub tuum praesidium" and first found in a Greek papyrus, c. 300, is the oldest prayer to Mary.

We turn to you for protection,
holy Mother of God.
Listen to our prayers
and help us in our needs.
Save us from every danger,
glorious and blessed Virgin.

Memorare

The "Memorare" is a sixteenth-century version of a fifteenth-century prayer. Claude Bernard (1588-1641) popularized the idea that the "Memorare" was written by Saint Bernard.

Remember, most loving Virgin Mary,
never was it heard
that anyone who turned to you for help
was left unaided.

Inspired by this confidence,
though burdened by my sins,

I run to your protection
for you are my mother.

Mother of the Word of God,
do not despise my words of pleading
but be merciful and hear my prayer.
Amen.

Mary, Help of Those in Need

This prayer was formerly the Magnificat antiphon from the Common of the Blessed Virgin Mary, Evening Prayer.

Holy Mary,
help those in need,
give strength to the weak,
comfort the sorrowful,
pray for God's people,
assist the clergy,
intercede for religious.
May all who seek your help
experience your unfailing protection.
Amen.

Prayer to Mary

Composed by Pope John Paul II for the Marian Year

Mother of the Redeemer,
[in this year dedicated to you,]
with great joy we call you blessed.

In order to carry out his providential plan of salvation,
God the Father chose you before the creation of the world.
You believed in his love and obeyed his word.

The Son of God desired you for his Mother
when he became man to save the human race.
You received him with ready obedience and undivided heart.

The Holy Spirit loved you as his mystical spouse
and he filled you with singular gifts.
You allowed yourself to be led
by his hidden and powerful action.

On the eve of the third Christian Millennium,
we entrust to you the Church
which acknowledges you and invokes you as Mother.
On earth you preceded the Church in the pilgrimage of faith:
comfort her in her difficulties and trials,
and make her always the sign and instrument
of intimate union with God
and of the unity of the whole human race.

To you, Mother of Christians,
we entrust in a special way
the peoples who are celebrating
[during the Marian Year]
the sixth Centenary or the Millennium
of their acceptance of the Gospel.
Their long history is profoundly marked by devotion to you.
Turn toward them your loving glance;
give strength to those who are suffering for the faith.

To you, Mother of the human family and of the nations,
we confidently entrust the whole of humanity,
with its hopes and fears.
Do not let it lack the light of true wisdom.
Guide its steps in the ways of peace.
Enable all to meet Christ,
the Way and the Truth and the Life.

Sustain us, O Virgin Mary, on our journey of faith
and obtain for us the grace of eternal salvation.
O clement, O loving, O sweet Mother of God
and our Mother, Mary!

The Angelus

The custom of saying the "Hail Mary" three times at the ringing of the bell of the evening goes back to the thirteenth century. Today, it is the custom to say the "Angelus" three times: in the morning, at noon, and in the evening.

The angel spoke God's message to Mary,
and she conceived of the Holy Spirit. *Hail Mary*

"I am the lowly servant of the Lord:
Let it be done to me according to your word." *Hail Mary*

And the Word became flesh
and lived among us. *Hail Mary*

Pray for us, holy Mother of God,
that we may become worthy of the promises of Christ.

Lord,
fill our hearts with your grace:
once, through the message of an angel
you revealed to us the incarnation of your Son;
now, through his suffering and death
lead us to the glory of his resurrection.
We ask this through Christ our Lord.
Amen.

Regina Caeli

From 1743, this twelfth-century antiphon has replaced the Angelus in the Easter Season.

Queen of heaven, rejoice, alleluia.
The Son you merited to bear, alleluia,
has risen as he said, alleluia.
Pray to God for us, alleluia.

Rejoice and be glad, O Virgin Mary, alleluia.
For the Lord has truly risen, alleluia.

God of life,
you have given joy to the world
by the resurrection of your Son, our Lord Jesus Christ.

Through the prayers of his mother, the Virgin Mary,
bring us to the happiness of eternal life.
We ask this through Christ our Lord.

Amen.

Litany of the Blessed Virgin Mary

The following litany is part of the newly approved *Order of Crowning an Image of the Blessed Virgin Mary.* The core of the litany lies in its explanation of Mary's Queenship.

Lord, have mercy.
Lord, have mercy.
Christ, have mercy.
Christ, have mercy.
Lord, have mercy.
Lord, have mercy.

God, our Father in heaven, *have mercy on us.*
God the Son, Redeemer of the world, *have mercy on us.*
God, the Holy Spirit, *have mercy on us.*
Holy Trinity, one God, *have mercy on us.*

Holy Mary, *pray for us.**
Holy Mother of God,
Most honored of virgins,

Chosen daughter of the Father,
Mother of Christ the King,
Glory of the Holy Spirit,

Virgin daughter of Zion,
Virgin poor and humble,
Virgin gentle and obedient,

Handmaid of the Lord,
Mother of the Lord,
Helper of the Redeemer,

Full of grace,
Fountain of beauty,
Model of virtue,

Finest fruit of the redemption,
Perfect disciple of Christ,
Untarnished image of the Church,

Woman transformed,
Woman clothed with the sun,
Woman crowned with stars,

Gentle Lady,
Gracious Lady,
Our Lady,

Joy of Israel,
Splendor of the Church,
Pride of the human race,

Advocate of grace,
Minister of holiness,
Champion of God's people,

Queen of love,
Queen of mercy,
Queen of peace,

Queen of angels,

* *Pray for us* is repeated after each invocation.

Queen of patriarchs and prophets,
Queen of apostles and martyrs,
Queen of confessors and virgins,
Queen of all saints,
Queen conceived without original sin,
Queen assumed into heaven,
Queen of all the earth,
Queen of heaven,
Queen of the universe,

Lamb of God, you take away the sins of the world; *spare us, O Lord.*
Lamb of God, you take away the sins of the world; *hear us, O Lord.*
Lamb of God, you take away the sins of the world; *have mercy on us.*

Pray for us, O glorious Mother of the Lord.
That we may become worthy of the promises of Christ.

God of mercy,
listen to the prayers of your servants
who have honored your handmaid Mary as mother and queen.
Grant that by your grace
we may serve you and our neighbor on earth
and be welcomed into your eternal kingdom.

We ask this through Christ our Lord.

The Litany of Loreto

The Litany of Loreto contains invocations that date back to the twelfth century. It was recorded in its present form (apart from a few additions by recent popes) at Loreto in 1558.

Lord, have mercy.
Lord, have mercy.
Christ, have mercy.
Christ, have mercy.
Lord, have mercy.
Lord, have mercy.

God, our Father in heaven, *have mercy on us.*
God the Son, Redeemer of the world, *have mercy on us.*
God, the Holy Spirit, *have mercy on us.*
Holy Trinity, one God, *have mercy on us.*

*Holy Mary, pray for us.**
Holy Mother of God,
Most honored of virgins,

Mother of Christ,
Mother of the Church,
Mother of Divine grace,
Mother most pure,

* *Pray for us* is repeated after each invocation

Mother of chaste love,
Mother and virgin,
Sinless Mother,
Dearest of mothers,
Model of motherhood,
Mother of good counsel,
Mother of our Creator,
Mother of our Savior,
Virgin most wise,
Virgin rightly praised,
Virgin rightly renowned,
Virgin most powerful,
Virgin gentle in mercy,
Faithful Virgin,
Mirror of justice,
Throne of wisdom,
Cause of our joy,
Shrine of the Spirit,

Glory of Israel,
Vessel of selfless devotion,
Mystical Rose,
Tower of David,
Tower of ivory,
House of gold,
Ark of the covenant,
Gate of heaven,
Morning Star,
Health of the sick,
Refuge of sinners,
Comfort of the troubled,
Help of Christians,

Queen of angels,
Queen of patriarchs and prophets,
Queen of apostles and martyrs,
Queen of confessors and virgins,
Queen of all saints,

Queen conceived without original sin,
Queen assumed into heaven,
Queen of the rosary,
Queen of peace,

Lamb of God, you take away the sins of the world; *have mercy on us.*
Lamb of God, you take away the sins of the world; *have mercy on us.*
Lamb of God, you take away the sins of the world; *have mercy on us.*

Pray for us, O holy Mother of God.
That we may become worthy of the promises of Christ.

Let us pray.

Eternal God,
let your people enjoy constant health in mind and body.
Through the intercession of the Virgin Mary
free us from the sorrows of this life
and lead us to happiness in the life to come.

Grant this through Christ our Lord.
Amen.

OTHER OUTSTANDING CATHOLIC BOOKS

DICTIONARY OF MARY—Newly revised and invaluable book that clearly sets forth the place of Mary in the Church and in the life of Catholics, her titles, authenticated apparitions, shrines, as well as Marian prayers and many other topics. **No. 367**

DAILY REFLECTIONS WITH MARY—By Rev. Rawley Myers. A beautifully illustrated and printed book that gives thirty-one prayerful Marian reflections plus a large selection of prayers to Our Lady. Every page is written out of deep love for Mary and inculcates a great devotion to her. **No. 372**

PRAYERS TO MARY—By Most Rev. Virgilio Noè. A beautiful book that includes prayers to Mary from various liturgies of the Church and Christians throughout the centuries as well as the more well-known prayers to Our Lady. Illustrated in full color. **No. 210**

TREASURY OF NOVENAS—By Rev. Lawrence G. Lovasik, S.V.D. More than forty popular Novenas carefully arranged for private prayer in accord with the Liturgical Year on the Feasts of Jesus, Mary, and favorite Saints. With color illustrations. **No. 345**

MARY DAY BY DAY—Introduction by Rev. Charles G. Fehrenbach, C.SS.R. Minute meditations for every day of the year, including a Scripture passage, a quotation from the Saints, and a concluding prayer. Printed in two colors with over 300 illustrations. **No. 180**

MARY MY HOPE—By Rev. Lawrence G. Lovasik, S.V.D. Popular book of devotions to Mary. Large type. Illustrated. **No. 365**

THE IMITATION OF MARY—By Rev. Alexander de Rouville, S.J. Companion volume to the *The Imitation of Christ*. Large type. Illustrated. **No. 330**

THE SECRET OF THE ROSARY—By St. Louis Grignion de Montfort. Modern translation of the classic work by the great Marian writer who nurtured St. John Paul II's devotion to our Blessed Mother. **No. 108**

PRAY THE ROSARY—By Rev. J. M. Lelen. The most popular, handy, purse-size Rosary booklet. Each Mystery is gloriously illustrated in full color with appropriate text. **No. 40**

---

www.catholicbookpublishing.com

ISBN 978-0-89942-450-7
90000
9 780899 424507